OVER THE
FARMER'S GATE

Roger Evans

Illustrations by Jonathan Heale

MERLIN UNWIN BOOKS

First published in Great Britain by Merlin Unwin Books, 2010
Reprinted 2010

Text © Roger Evans 2010
Illustrations © Jonathan Heale 2010

Published by:
Merlin Unwin Books Ltd
Palmers House
7 Corve Street
Ludlow
Shropshire SY8 1DB
U.K.

www.merlinunwin.co.uk

Designed and set in Bembo 11pt by Merlin Unwin
Printed in Great Britain by MPG Biddles Ltd

ISBN 978 1 906122 25 6

CONTENTS

To all of my family

Spring

I'M A DAIRY FARMER and I live and farm in a particularly beautiful part of the country. People often say how lucky I am to live around here and that I probably take it for granted.

A day never passes when I don't appreciate what I have around me, and in some ways this book offers an opportunity to share how and where I live and what I see about me. I see myself as a privileged spectator, observing what goes on among the people, wildlife, the animals I live and work with and a countryside that I cherish.

I work long hours, often on repetitive work and watching wildlife is often a welcome distraction. I've got this mobile hide that I use as a vantage point. It's very unobtrusive; birds and animals have become used to seeing it about, it's got glass all around, it's green so it blends in and it's called a tractor.

It's a life and death struggle for the wildlife out there. You can watch something flourish but there's usually a predator lurking in the background. When I see an aggressive species gaining the upper hand I long to intervene, to provide some balance. Balance is a theme I will return to often.

And then there are the people. Sometimes I use the tractor to creep up on them as well. The people around here have changed beyond belief as more seek to live in this sort of area.

There was a time, when driving the tractor through the village, that if I saw a stranger I would slow down and stare at them. These days I can see lots of people I don't know but they all seem to know each other and they're staring at me.

Thirty or forty years ago, there were a couple of farms within the village and the movement of stock and farm vehicles within the village was an everyday occurrence. The farms are gone now, and the buildings have become homes.

I kept a flock of sheep for many years and their summer grazing was the other side of the village, and we had to bring them home regularly for shearing and dipping. Farming life is full of ironies and sheep are particularly adept at irony. They used to graze a succession of fields, the furthest parts of which were nearly a mile away from the roadside gate. The sheep would be in what an auctioneer would describe as 'flock ages', meaning that at one end of the scale you would have the young fit ewes you had bought the previous autumn – yearling ewes – and at the other end you would have the old granny ewes.

Sheep are a bit like humans: the young ones could go drinking and dancing all night, the old ones are getting a bit broad in the beam, starting to lose their teeth, and are definitely unfit. The irony was that when you went to fetch the flock home, the yearling ewes all seemed to be close to the road while the old ewes would be at the other end of their range.

I would put the dog around, very gently, but the effect was always the same, a breakneck gallop to the road, the old ewes trying to keep up with their lambs, who thought all this was great fun. When you opened the gate, the yearling ewes would be off down the road.

Eventually, out through the gate would come the granny ewes, puffing and blowing. There was nothing cruel about this, but if you're 65 you shouldn't go jogging with 18-year-olds.

By the time we would get to the village some of the old ewes would be starting to struggle. Just when you had about 10 cars behind you, some of them would flop down in the road for a rest.

This would present a dilemma, but there were sanctuaries you could use. We used to pop half a dozen into the school playground, a couple in the phone box and local people would recognise whose they were and know that you'd be back with the van to pick them up later. These days the RSPCA would be there long before you could get back with the van.

The sheep have long gone. I kept the land on for a few years and used to graze my in-calf heifers there. I used to walk them there in the spring and back in the autumn. When you are taking heifers through the village, past an open plan garden, and they've been shut in a building all winter and there's a nice bite of grass on somebody's lawn, they can take a bit of getting off and back on to the road. The heifer that's gone into the greenhouse can take a bit longer.

I used to know the names of all the children who attended the village school and names of all the young mums who took them there. I don't any more. Times change. There was a time when I used to take 15 children to swimming class in a Morris Oxford, with three in the boot, and only two were mine. I don't do that any more either.

* * *

AT LONG last, a friend has come to set some mole traps in the garden. I've tried to catch them with little success (well, none really) and my grandsons complain that the molehills spoil the football and that cricket is completely out of the question.

We've now caught one, but there are three new areas of mole activity. The dog tries to help by digging for them but this doesn't help the sporting activity and as far as I know, he's less successful than me.

Next time I buy a lawnmower I will have one with a blade on the front like a bulldozer to level the molehills.

Round here they are called 'unts' (moles, that is) and a molehill is called an unty tump.

* * *

THERE has been a lot of publicity recently about farmers being subsidised with what is called a single farm payment. The publicity centred on the fact that the money was due at the end of last year but the Government, for a variety of reasons, had failed to pay it out until recently. Without labouring the late-payment problem, the publicity it generated did flag up the subsidy issue and, as a farmer, I was on the end of quite a lot of teasing about receiving hand-outs, particularly from people involved in other businesses. Most of the teasing was thinly veiled sarcasm; I'm quite good at sarcasm myself but resisted the temptation, because deep down I would prefer not to receive this money. I would rather receive adequate returns from the market place, but I don't.

Historically, money was directed towards the production of food, resulting in the food mountains that have long gone and now exist only in the minds of some politicians.

We are now paid to look after the countryside and the environment, which we do, and I hope that something of my own caring and responsibility comes across in this book. The reality is that few farm businesses would survive without this money. My milk at the moment is worth about 17½p a litre. Ten years ago it was worth 25p. Ironically, milk prices are under huge pressure at the moment and are likely to go down even further.

We produce broiler chicken here as well as milk. I love to see a new batch of chicks running about on nice, clean sawdust. When they are ready to go you can hardly walk between them. I would like to be able to reduce stocking density but if I did we couldn't compete with imports. A friend of mine criticises the way we rear our poultry yet enthuses about being able to buy a ready-cooked chicken for £3.

I have to go to London on the train about once a month and there's a farm we pass that hasn't been 'farmed' for several years. To start with, it looked like several fields of dead grass and weeds; now it's all briars and thorn bushes. Soon it will be an impassable eyesore. I don't think the public want that.

In the pub one night, a local garage owner was waxing eloquent about farmers' payments. I kept my own counsel but couldn't help thinking that if I could have for my milk what I was getting 10 years ago, and he was charging for his petrol what he was getting 10 years ago and all the other products I buy were at the same level, he could have my single farm payment with pleasure.

* * *

WE'VE GOT quite a lot of cats about this farm. There are two that are sort of house cats that live in a utility room. We can call on these two if we get any unwelcome furry visitors with long tails in the house, which old farmhouses often do.

And there are the other cats. I don't know how many there are, they seem to come and go. Two years ago, there were 22. We give them milk every day, so that's when I count them.

I prefer to think of them as feral cats because farm assurance seems to think I should care for them. You can't touch them because they never come near enough. I suspect that if you did, you could lose some fingers.

There's a beautiful grey, half-grown kitten that lives up with the young calves. I give it food and milk every day because I would like to tame it, catch it and give it to my granddaughter for a pet. Most of them are ginger, a legacy of a ferocious ginger tomcat that used to visit here at one time. If you met him in a doorway he would snarl at you and it would be a question of who had the bottle to keep going. I don't like the ginger cats because they remind me of him.

We've got a couple of tabby cats. One is very old with a bent ear but she's always working away. We've got four or five nice black ones as well. What we haven't got are rats. We used to have a lot of wrens about but I suspect the cats have had them as well.

Then there are the dogs. If not on farming duties, the dogs busy themselves keeping the cats busy. We have a bearded collie who was brought to work the cattle and he can do the whole thing, the outrun, the fetch and the pen, but only with cats. He spends his day working with the cats. The cats, for their part, being fiercely independent, take very little notice of him. So when he thinks he's got a couple cornered up in a 'pen', it's only because that's where those particular cats have decided to go. Sometimes he is joined by Mert our border collie and when I hear prolonged barking and I go to investigate, it is always because a new cat or a new kitten has turned up.

It has always intrigued me that the dogs can differentiate between new cats and their regular cats. At night, the corgi lives in the kitchen, the bearded collie runs loose (I wouldn't be that bothered if he ran away) and the border collie is chained up. Dogs are a bit like young boys, leave them to their own devices and they will get up to mischief.

The border collie lives in what used to be a henhouse situated in what used to be a walled kitchen garden. He has a nice long chain so he can go into the henhouse or quite a way outside. In the summer, wet or dry, he sleeps outside. Last week, I tidied up his shed and gave him a thick wad of nice clean straw to sleep on. Next morning, when it was still very dark, I went to release him to come with me to fetch the cows. He had made himself a cosy nest in the straw and at first glance in the torchlight he looked a lot bigger than usual.

The reason? There, curled up with him in the same warm hollow, were three black cats. They were so close together that you couldn't tell where the cats finished and the dog started. An hour later there was a standoff between a collection of dogs and a collection of cats around the milk dish. Confrontation by day, cuddles at night, bit like being married.

* * *

I HAVEN'T seen the keeper for about a month; he's been busy with the lambing at the farm where he works full-time. But that's all finished now and he's done his spring sowing so his zest and enthusiasm are focused back on to his part-time job as a gamekeeper.

We have a meeting planned today, Saturday morning. Every year I allow him to grow two acres of game cover on my land and today we meet to decide if I will allow the arrangement to continue, and for how much.

He's fairly confident on the continuation issue but the cost is a bit more sensitive. I often think that members of shooting syndicates expect the shoot to run on a shoestring.

Shooting is very expensive anyway but I had a theory when I played rugby that whatever it cost to go on some trip or other would actually cost you double that, because your wife would spend the same amount on herself and, in reality, there wasn't much you could say about it. I am sure that the same applies to shooting.

'How much rent will you want this year?'

I'm straight to the main issue, I haven't time to hang about today as my Discovery has a poorly clutch and I'm in my son's car and he's off to play rugby at 11 o'clock. 'I want £1,000 up-front and a 200-bird day's shooting for me and my friends.'

I get one of his thin smiles. That's way over the top but people say I have a very convincing style when it comes to winding them up. We eventually agree on £100 more than last year. He doesn't seem over-pleased but I'm sure the shoot expected to pay more, so why disappoint them?

That done, he moves on.

'We were foxing last night and I reckon there were over 40 of your hares in that wood.'

I've seen hares about, but not that many.

'Tom Lewis was standing in that corner by the stile and there were 18 went past him.'

Now I know the Tom Lewis in question, and his tendency to exaggerate, so there were probably four or five.

'You like your hares and I keep an eye on them for you.'

Slowly but surely they've become 'my' hares – and it's true, I do like them. It's just that I suspect that if another tenant complains to the keeper about hare damage they will be Roger Evans' hares that are causing the trouble.

'Many foxes about?' I ask innocently.

'A few.'

Strange that he knows, or he reckons he knows, exactly how many hares there are about, but he's not going to tell me how many foxes they shot.

* * *

I WAS PUTTING some fertiliser on the winter wheat the other day and I spotted a tiny lèveret scuttling along on an adjacent tramline.

When we drill a field we miss drills on a regular basis so that we have somewhere to drive the tractor in subsequent operations without damaging the crop.

Leverets travel down these tramlines; scuttle is the right word because they travel flat to the ground, trying to keep out of sight.

As I watched, a buzzard swooped in and carried the unfortunate leveret away in one easy motion. Left me a bit sad really, but life and death are all around in the springtime. I've seen this happen before, but never this close.

Spring has finally burst upon us in just a few days. We suffered a really raw day with a biting east wind and temperatures stuck at three degrees centigrade and the next day it was 18 degrees. In just a few days since then I have seen my first swallow, my first house martin and heard the cuckoo. There is a suggestion within the family that I hear the cuckoo all year round.

Nothing epitomises spring more than the sound of larks on a sunny day. We are well blessed with larks around here and in the last few days of warm weather they have really been making up for lost time.

★ ★ ★

SOMETIMES I don't know whether to laugh or cry. Given the choice I prefer to laugh - there's plenty to make you cry as a dairy farmer - so when something is within your own remit, a chuckle is better than tears. I was moving some dry cows in a trailer. They'd just completed lactation and were now going off for a couple of months to our other land. A couple of months to recuperate, replenish body reserves, off concrete on to a nice grassy field, a time, as it were, to use my grandchildren's jargon, to chill out. Because the lane is a bit narrow where I was dropping them off, I have to park the trailer at right angles to the gateway so that as the cows come out of the trailer they have to turn 90 degrees into the field. This shouldn't be any big deal; with me standing in a strategically suitable place and the sight of a grassy field in the other direction, it should be, grandchildren jargon again, a no-brainer. The only slight negative to this carefully planned scenario is that there are already nine in-calf heifers in the field.

As I pull up they are all lying down at the far end of the field so that shouldn't be a problem. As I park up, the cows in the trailer, three of them, decide to re-establish some sort of pecking order. This apparently involves a lot of pushing and shoving, probably a bit of a fight, and lots and lots of clatter and an element of trailer bouncing.

If you are an in-calf heifer lying down, chewing your cud, this sort of commotion is irresistible, so you jump smartly to your feet and race up the field to the gate just as fast as you can. Getting the cows out of the trailer is now just a bit more difficult.

There is an unavoidable sequence to events now. I have to open the field gate first whatever I do, and then run smartly to the trailer, let down the tailboard, open the two stock gates within the trailer and get back into my strategic position just as quickly as I can. Alas, smartly and quickly are not smartly and quickly enough and two of the in-calf heifers are out of the field and away into the distance.

People sometimes ask me what it's like getting old. Well, it's OK just as long as you don't try to run anywhere. So I've got two heifers about a hundred yards away now and seven heifers and three dry cows in the field and quite a dilemma. But help is at hand. Under the tailboard of the trailer is Mert my border collie.

He just loves moving cattle in the trailer and at loading and unloading, he is always under the ramp. Apparently, this is a good place from which to bite a wayward ankle; mostly it is cattle ankles but it could just as easily be mine. So eager is he to get under the trailer that there's a good chance he could get run over one day but that's his problem.

But now is his big chance to shine and he takes it. 'Get on by Mert,' I cry, pointing down the lane at the two disappearing heifers. And he does, he does get on by, he goes into the field and fetches the other 10 cattle as well. The only plus here is that they set off in the same direction as the other two.

The first two heifers are out of sight now but Mert is still my only chance unless I start to make frantic mobile phone calls home for help. Not keen to admit that I can't unload three cows into a field on my own I try once more: 'Get on by Mert'.

And once again he does. He's off down the lane, past the big bunch and out of sight after the other two. Moments later they are all coming back towards me, the two that caused the trouble at some speed, high-stepping it like Welsh cobs at a show. Obviously there's been a bit of ankle-nipping going on. Into the field and shut the gate, job done.

My relief is huge. The next junction down the lane is a place we call Five Turnings, for fairly obvious reasons. Goodness knows where they would all have ended up if they'd got that far.

The fuss I make of the dog is at a level he's not experienced before and he's so grateful that, returning home, he tries to sit on my lap instead of his usual place between the two front seats, and I can't get the seat belt around the two of us.

But it's not quite 'job done' – there's another load of four cows to move yet. This time I take a bit more care. I back the trailer a bit nearer to the gate so that I have a bit less of a gap to cover. The cattle already in the field are by the gate but I think I've got everything covered. Mert is in his usual place under the trailer. I open the gate and leap to the trailer ramp. On the previous occasion opening the trailer smartly wasn't quick enough. This time my 'leap' is lacking in speed as well, because without a word from me the dog is into the field and has the 12 cattle out on the road quicker than I can say the F word.

With an air of resignation I let the four cows out of the trailer to join them. At least I have them all in the same place, even if it's the wrong place. And the dog? He's away down the lane, still unbidden, and fetches all the cattle back with an air of self-satisfaction.

There's 16 cattle in this group now and it takes some bottle for a dog to pass them in a narrow lane, stop them, turn them and bring them back. I know that, the dog knows that, and he presents himself for the fuss he'd had at the previous incident with some pride.

He gets his reward and, as I drive back, I look across at him and wonder just who is in charge here. I'm still not sure of the answer. I get back into the yard.

'Everything OK?' my son asks.

'Yes fine.' I don't tell anyone I've just been on an adventure.

* * *

THE CALVES being born here now were fathered by the Belgian Blue bull we bought last year. There is a good demand for this beef-cross calf, so we are hoping the revenue will help to alleviate milk prices, which are on the downward slide.

We try to give all our calves a good start in life. They spend the first 24 hours with their mum and then they are put with all the other fresh-calved cows in our loose-housed shed, where there is plenty of room and nice fresh straw to lie on twice a day.

In theory, they can stay here for several days if they behave themselves and it is luxury living while it lasts. It's the nearest they will get to post-natal care with BUPA.

Twice a day these cows go down to the parlour to be milked and it can be very difficult parting calves from mums to achieve this, especially if half the cows in the group think it's their calf.

Having persuaded the cows out of the shed, you have to persuade the calves to stay there. But usually this can be done because it's a natural instinct for a calf to go and lie on its own while its mother isn't about. This can be a real problem when calves are born outside in the summer, as they will secrete themselves away in clumps of nettles and the like and you can spend ages looking for them.

Anyway, with luck the calves in the shed will go and lie by the walls until mother returns from the milking parlour, which will be only 15 minutes or so. If they go and lie quietly, you can file the mothers back there uninterrupted after being milked. But it doesn't always work like that. Sometimes, at a signal I cannot detect, four or five calves will kick their heels up, frolic around the shed a couple of times and then it's off down the yard at a hundred miles an hour causing chaos everywhere they go. It's then that they get taken from mother.

We had a good calf that would go and lie down at milking time, its mother would leave it for the short time without any fuss, and so it stayed there for about a week and grew and thrived. One day I went to get the group of cows to milk them and there was no sign of the calf. The mother was lying there chewing her cud, completely content. I walked around the shed again – there are 40 cows in this group, so I could have missed it. But experience told me where it was. I got the cow up and there was the calf, cosy and warm, flat and dead. Mother had been sitting on top of it like a broody hen trying to hatch some eggs. Sometimes animals will contrive to die despite your best efforts.

We had a cow once that lay on three calves in succession; she'd killed them as soon as they were born and before we ever saw them alive.

* * *

WHEN WE came to live here, in 1964, there was a man living in one of the cottages who had worked on the farm for 47 years.

He used to tell me that his first job here, with others, was to construct a grass tennis court by the farmhouse. They had to excavate by hand into the sloping garden and then work a fine tilth on a nearby field and cart the top two or three inches of fine soil back with horse and cart to create the seedbed they needed.

If ever you read that fine book *Farmer's Glory* by A G Street, you will find that the playing of tennis was an important part of the life of a yeoman farmer, whose lifestyle brought them close to the leisured classes.

This was quite readily achieved if you had lots of staff and paid them just enough, but only just. We've never used this part of our lawn as a tennis court but it has seen lots of use as a football pitch and I have constructed goalposts at one end so that my grandsons can practise their goal-kicks for rugby, as well.

This year, large parts of the lawn resemble a war zone, as the lawn has been taken over by moles. The trouble is, I've never been any good at catching them. Until this week, the only mole I have 'caught' for years was when I spent the whole of a sunny evening sitting in the garden reading the Sunday papers with a shotgun in my lap.

I've tried all sorts of traps, smoke bombs, pills, windmills in bottles, the lot. Expert mole-catchers use traps but they never worked for me.

My heifers are away on another farm and the manager there is always catching moles successfully. Eventually, the lure of a can of cider and £5-a-mole brought him to our garden.

He surveyed the scene of destruction quite nonchalantly and then found a run along the wall at one side and another along the fence and he put two traps down.

I couldn't see how he detected these runs but it was done in no time at all. Next morning there was a mole in each trap so I re-laid them and the next day there were two more.

I've not caught one for several days now but there are still new molehills every morning, albeit at a reduced level of activity.

I had a man working here many years ago who was good at catching moles. He claimed to know something of a mole's psyche. He had a theory that it was impossible to catch a mole in the normal course of events; they were too clever and could easily detect a trap. You could catch them only when they were running away and a mole will run away only from mating and fighting. He didn't use the word mating; he used another word, a word that connected with fighting as an example of alliteration. He didn't know that alliteration existed but it had a certain eloquence to it. How he knew all that, goodness only knows. We can see what the birds of the air and the beasts of the field get up to, but what goes on underground is more of a mystery.

It wasn't for me to tell him he'd made it all up – the way he told it, it was a good story and anyway, he could catch moles.

I had a good look at the first one I caught. They are quite remarkable little creatures, their little 'hands' able to dig away all that soil. I bear them no ill will; it's just that I don't need them on my lawn.

Truth be told, we don't need them in fields, either. Too many molehills in a field and your silage can be contaminated with soil and the cattle can die of listeria. Not a lot going for it, really, old mole.

★ ★ ★

THERE ARE only two sounds to be heard at this time of the morning. The most obvious one is the non-stop tinkling of the cow bell attached to my brown Swiss cow.

It's a constant in our lives now; you can hear it as you go out of the kitchen door, ringing to the cow's slightest movement, even, it seems, as she breathes.

I like to hear it, but my wife thinks it's cruel. 'What,' she says, 'if the cow doesn't like a bell ringing around her neck night and day, 24/7?' She has a point, and I may take it off and put it on another cow to give her a break.

There's another noise and I like to hear that as well – the sound of barn owls hunting. If you see one close to, even if it is stuffed and in a case, you wonder if you ever saw such beautiful plumage.

Some people around here call owls 'hullards'. I've no idea why – perhaps it's a sort of dialect name – but it doesn't stop there. If your name is Howells, and there are a goodly number of Howells about this area, Jimmy Howells, for example, can end up being called Jimmy Hullard!

I used to be in a group of pheasant shooters and one of the members used to bring a guest regularly who was ultra-conscious of a step he mistakenly thought he had taken up the social ladder, and he used to attach an 'H' to all sorts of words as he tried to posh himself up.

We would often see owls when we shot away in the woods. The first time he saw one it was a 'howl', and that's what they all became after that.

Just to complete the bird theme, when my brother first started school there were two girls in his class who caught his eye, one called Hazel Pigeon and one called Hazel Dove. He thought they were sisters. But then life has always been a struggle for him.

* * *

IT IS OFTEN brought home to me the strange phenomena of people in towns and cities who don't talk to each other. They may not know them, but surely they see the same people every day on the same train, so what's the problem?

Talking to the people I meet daily is an important part of my life and I struggle to imagine a life without it.

But sometimes it can be a bit of a nuisance if you are in a rush. Once, memorably, I was sent into our small local town on Christmas Eve to get some chestnuts. I came back three hours later with one chestnut!

This week I had a similar experience. I've been busy with my dairy co-op work lately and although a recent day involved a drive to the top end of Lancashire, there were a couple of jobs of my own I needed to do before I went.

So I set off a couple of hours early and my first stop was the shoe shop. The shop keeper is in his late 60s, owns three or four shops, does a bit of farming, and is a third-generation cobbler and proud of it.

I drew his attention to the black shoes I was wearing with a broken shoelace and a sole showing a bit of a gap from the upper.

We had a bit of banter about the shoes still being under guarantee, but eventually he told me to get them off while he put soles and heels on them.

I pulled up a chair and watched him at his work. It took him about 40 minutes and in this time we had a good chat about farming and shoe-mending.

He told me how he spent most of his National Service mending army boots. He still has examples about his shop of footwear of yesteryear, including those old football boots with leather nail-in studs, and hob-nail boots for a small child, all of which he made himself.

I'm always telling him he should make more of this memorabilia with a small display area within the shop but he doesn't seem to be motivated to do that.

Throughout his life he envied farmers, thinking they made a

fortune, so he bought two farms. He's not found it as easy as he thought, but he still thinks he's missing a trick somewhere.

Job done, I drove a couple of hundred yards up the street to get my new glasses. There was a time when my glasses were quite safe within the breast pocket of my shirt, where they lived with my mobile phone. I seem to have several shirts now without this important accessory and my glasses became seriously damaged in my trouser pocket.

They've spent two weeks held together with Sellotape and I've had to drive with my head tilted on one side to keep my world level.

My daughter suggested holding them together with Elastoplast, saying: 'Then you'll really look like Jack Duckworth.'

My new glasses had arrived and the optometrist and her assistant were all over me as they determined that the new glasses fitted correctly.

I found the close proximity to these two women a bit disconcerting, because when I say close, they really were close. It's probably because I'd showered and got clean 'going out' clothes on, whereas when I came to have my eyes tested I was in my working clothes and rather 'mucky'.

It is not such an enjoyable experience when they touch me for £260 for the new glasses and the bits they have bought to mend my old glasses, which will now become my working glasses.

As I went out of the shop I tried to evaluate the elements of cost that I had to pay for the traces of perfume that still linger about me, so I decided that the glasses were quite reasonable.

Across the road from the opticians is the florist and the florist, who I know well, is outside the shop talking to another woman, who I also know.

Spotting me washed and tidy they came across and wanted to know where I was off to. I took the opportunity to get the florist to come and turn the volume up on my new sat-nav. I could do it on the old sat-nav but haven't worked out how to do it on this.

The florist remarks on the nice female Irish voice I have on it. I told her I chose it because it reminds me of the lady who kept the pub in Ballykissangel – I think I'm falling in love with the lady on the sat-nav.

The florist told me she'd done the flowers for four funerals already this week but my love for the sat-nav lady was about the saddest thing she'd heard. Suitably put down, I finally set off on my journey.

* * *

IT WAS A lovely sunny Sunday morning and the sumptuous breakfast I prepared – beans on toast – had been consumed and I was back out in the yard.

There's only me about at the moment and my first job was to let out the group of lower yielding cows who, for a week now, have been going out in the daytime to lie in the field in front of our house. This left two separate groups of high yielders very envious, and I could see them contemplating a bit of gate-jumping as they watched their colleagues make their way out.

It was such a nice day (it could easily have been May) so I decided to divert the low yielders on to a fresh field of grass. I let one group of high yielders on to the field in front of the house and the other group of high yielders out into what used to be a two-acre orchard.

None of them needed any bidding to embrace this new regime and within just a few minutes the buildings were empty of cows.

One group was soon busy grazing and the two others were lying down, soaking up the sunshine.

It was the first time for more than six months that the buildings had been empty of cattle and there was strangeness about it.

There's been births, deaths, cows mooing against gates, ringing their bloody bells, and now just silence.

I've noticed this before in a lambing shed. Two months of activity and then it's all gone. Just the debris is left; bits of wool, the empty isolation pens, a dead lamb slung over a gate. The flock, and their incessant bleating, move on to the next stage of their annual cycle and, like the cows, they are pleased, as it takes them back to the fields where they belong.

★ ★ ★

THE FIRST bunch of cows we milk in the morning – they are the group we optimistically call 'high yielders' – have to be fetched home by torchlight.

The second group is usually further away and fetched in a sort of half-light, not quite light, but, then again, not really dark enough to take the torch, especially if you'd rather fetch them with your hands in your pockets.

When I arrive at the gate of their usual night field – they have the run of 12 acres going up to the wood – I can only see the very white cows. More importantly, I can't see the dog.

Mert can be a bit hard on cows but he is also easy to stop. I send him off into the gloom and watch carefully. Up by the wood fence, a white cows bolts about 20 yards so now I know where he is. 'Steady.' After that, they all come in a very leisurely fashion, many of them pausing as they cross the stream to have a drink.

I like to see cows drinking out of a stream. The water is provided free by gravity – it doesn't cost over a pound a cubic metre like the water in the troughs on the yard. Within the 10 minutes or so it takes to clear the field, it has become perceptibly lighter and I can take one quick scan around the field to make sure it is clear of cows. All around the field are little columns of vapour marking where the cows have had their first pee of the day or their first number two.

We, the cows and I, make our way home up a stone track that is softly carpeted with thatching straw, which I had salvaged from a cottage which was being re-thatched. It makes for very comfortable walking for men and beasts. The dog is thirty yards away. He doesn't use the track – it's bordered by an electric fence and he's inadvertently brushed it with his tail on occasions.

Among the straw are a lot of the hazel stick spars that had been used to hold the straw in place on the roof, but that's not all. There are just a few pieces of a newspaper that must have found its way into the roof at the last thatching. I pick up a piece to read as we make our way slowly home. It's not easy to read because I think some mice have read it first. It is dated 1 February 1954. It tells me, among other things, that the country is carpeted with thick snow and that there is more on the way.

The big political issue of the day, as in really big, was should Britain trade with Germany or Japan? To be fair, this is less than ten years after the end of World War II, but it's a question that seems bizarre today. I'm writing this and you are reading it surrounded by products of both countries in abundance. I can, I am told, buy a new English electric cooker for £37 12 shillings and sixpence. I bet that was a lot of money in 1954. Surprising what you can find out in the early morning just fetching the cows.

I shut the gate behind the cows and sneak off for a second cup of tea. Around the taller trees in the garden a buzzard and two carrion crows are involved in one of their perpetual dogfights. Both species seem to spend the hours of daylight in a constant squabble to the extent that I wonder if they ever manage to get anything else done, like breeding, laying and feeding their young.

The dogs make their way back up the yard. It's not much fun being a dog at our place at the moment. A couple of months ago we had about twenty sleek, well-fed cats about the place. I think we still have the same number but you can't see them all. A lot of them developed big fat tummies that someone as perceptive as me diagnosed as pregnancy.

Since then, they have secreted themselves away to give birth. There are cats under things, among things, down holes, in stacks of bales, under implements, everywhere. And where the cats are, there are also kittens. I haven't seen any kittens yet but I know they are there; the big tummies have all gone. For your unsuspecting dog it's a difficult time. Quite innocently, making its way about the yard on some doggy business or other, your dog is likely to walk past a stack of bales only to be violently attacked by a spitfire of a protective cat. I've even seen a dog fast asleep in some warm, sheltered corner when a cat comes into view and leaps on to the unsuspecting dog, spitting, clawing and biting. What sort of awakening is that?

Predominant among the busy sounds of birds in the morning is the sound of wood pigeons. I really like to hear them. There is something of calm and contentment about it. Traditionally, it's called cooing but I don't think that really describes it. But as I can't come up with any better description, cooing it will have to be.

Our AI man described the sound as being that of a working man's cuckoo. He's already heard a cuckoo. I've not, but then he gets about a fair bit more than me, into softer warmer climes than we enjoy, into places like Herefordshire for example.

If there is a bird sound that I put way out in front of all others it's the sound of the curlew. There's a pair busy about the area again this year which is such good news. Curlews reappeared around here last year, as I may have reported, after an absence of several years. They bred and have now returned.

What does disappoint and concern me is the absence of

lapwings in the area. There are lots of suitable sites around here that you would assume would be perfect breeding areas, mostly on set-aside fields.

Lapwings seem to prefer open ground to nest on – and a partially worked, set-aside field would be perfect – and then the opportunity to take their chicks nearer to water after about three days. I know of two sites in the area that hosted lapwings – one had nine pairs last year. The local wildlife trust took over the sites and fenced them in. The carrion crows and buzzard used the fence posts as perches and cleared up every egg.

Still, they know best. After all, we are only simple farmers.

★ ★ ★

AS THE YEAR goes on there are milestones that mark the passing of the days. Now I can switch all the yard lights off before we finish milking in the mornings.

Every year, the Canada geese arrive at dawn. You don't always see them arrive, but you always hear them. They come to nest on the little island in the pond in front of our house.

Sometimes, half a dozen come at the same time and they fight for two or three days for the nesting site.

In goose terms, the island is a 'one up, one down', so there's room for only one nest. This year, a single pair have arrived and I did see them fly in. They swept in with loud calls as though proclaiming ownership of the island, the field and the territory.

Like the season itself, they are late this year. They usually come in mid-February, which puts them nearly a month late, but the spring around here is about the same.

Our daffodils still aren't out and it intrigues me that plant and animal life – or in this case bird life – is attuned to the same sort of timing that adjusts itself to the vagaries of the weather.

The pair have been here only a couple of days and already the female is sitting on what she presumably calls a nest, laying her eggs. It's all very interesting.

In due course there will be the young gulls to watch, too, and then they'll fly back to the lake a mile away, from where they came.

But what we really want are some swans.

* * *

I'VE ALWAYS categorised myself as being pretty 'cool', laid back, fairly unflappable. Not as laid back as my son, though. If he were more laid back he would fall over.

But there are a few times of the year when I admit that I do become a bit more 'on edge', and as I write today, we are right in the middle of one of those periods.

It's the time of year to get our maize in. It's a very important crop to us, it's expensive to grow and it's critical to get it right. Last year, we had to abandon 17 acres of maize to the wet weather and there was a very serious knock-on cost to our business for the rest of the winter. So that makes this year's crop all the more important and puts me just that bit more 'on the edge'.

I have a date in mind of 11 or 12 May for drilling here. We are just on the margins of growing maize because of our height above sea level and we also suffer late frosts. Maize is a tall and vigorous crop but it won't compete with weeds, bad weather, and even the shadows cast by the trees across the road leave their mark.

We put a lot of farmyard manure under maize, it loves it, and we did that part of the operation ahead of schedule. So when I put the plough on, I was pretty cool about it all because I would be more than a week ahead of time to plough and work down the fields. I actually enjoy ploughing, if it's going OK, and I was looking forward to a couple of days on my own surrounded by the beauty of the spring countryside and the opportunity to observe the wildlife.

Being on my own is the best company I can have. The dog would come with me in the cab if I let him but it's a long old day for him, bumping along on the cab floor. He would follow me up and down the field all day if I let him as well, but, then again, he might not – it's springtime and at the moment he is much given to carnal thoughts.

So off I go and, in my mind's eye, I have a picture of endless shiny furrows falling smoothly away from the plough, a flock of seagulls following me up and down the field – an idyllic scene (I can almost feel a poem coming on), while on the radio the rest of the world is queuing up around an accident on the M6 near Birmingham.

But life can let you down. There were some furrows falling away, but not many. Problems with the plough, problems with the tractor, there was more time spent with my hands on spanners than on the steering wheel. I had gone from cool to very tetchy in a short time.

By mid-afternoon I had ploughed, to use a technical term with which a few of you will be familiar, bugger all. A piece on the plough broke (it's surprising how long it takes to go six miles to fetch a spare part), but then all fell into place and away we went.

So I started to relax and look about me, wondering where all the wildlife was – there was none to be seen. Not even the compulsory flock of seagulls.

We're a long way from the sea here but there are local seagulls that live on a pool. Local legend has it that they have never been to the seaside and therefore are not to be trusted.

To get back somewhere nearer to the schedule I had in my mind, I ploughed on into the evening. There was nothing to be seen and then suddenly, at about eight o'clock, standing on the ploughed ground just ten yards away, was a solitary lapwing.

He, she, whatever, didn't move and as I passed and re-passed,

I started to agonise over the possibility that I'd ploughed a nest. I'd been ploughing 20 acres in a 40-acre field. The other 20 acres will be left with last year's stubble for wild birds to nest in. It would be ironic if this lapwing chose the wrong 20 acres to nest on. Then its mate turned up and the pair spent their time on the unploughed area. As far as I could make out, I'd disturbed the pair of lapwings and a pair of skylarks.

The lapwings are more of a concern. They are the first pair I've seen lately, and we've plenty of skylarks.

I drove home late in the evening hoping that there would be time for them to make a fresh start.

With time to make up to get back to my schedule, it was a very early start the next morning. I set off to plough just as it got light. First on my list was a lovely white owl, still busy working the hedgerows, I could easily have stopped to watch it if I'd had the time.

The pairs of lapwings and skylarks were still there but before long a heron arrived and was soon gorging itself on worms.

Then down the valley, effortlessly gliding like stealth bombers came a pair of red kites. They circled me a couple of times, not looking for food but to check on the quality of the ploughing. The ploughing isn't bad if you don't look too closely at what I did at the start, and off they went down the valley. They exuded aloofness and superiority as they went on their way.

* * *

EVERY year we try to get away for a few days' holiday in May. The holidays seem to get shorter and shorter as we try to sandwich them between our B&B guests departing and the next ones arriving.

We always seem to have guests leaving the day we go and new ones arriving the day we get home. It becomes quite critical within our own travel arrangements about what sort of risers the departing ones are, and, if they are a bit slow in the mornings; will it affect our own travel arrangements?

You sometimes sit there, bags packed and in the car, listening to them taking a leisurely breakfast, to which they are perfectly entitled, and you feel like going in and asking: 'Well are you going to eat that sausage or not?'

I sometimes think we've got our priorities all wrong, but we seem to manage.

This year we went to Ireland, somewhere we've been lots of times before, but decided this time to go to the north.

We've never been to the north before and very beautiful it is, too, I recommend it. There's a lovely ride that follows the coast north of Larne, I think it's the Antrim coast, and, late afternoon one day, we stopped in a small village for a cup of tea.

Well, you can have tea at home, can't you, so we decided to have some Guinness. We were on our second, or was it our third, when a big man in a black suit comes in and starts drinking at the bar.

There's me, busy at my people-watching, and I see that he is vigorously chewing at something he keeps pulling out of his pocket. He's a bit of a people-watcher as well and before long he's watching me watching him.

At first I think he's not best pleased, but he plunges his hand in his pocket and thrusts out a big handful of what looks like dark brown chewing tobacco, and says: 'Want some?'

I ask him what it is. His accent is very strong but I eventually find out it is called 'dulse' and it is dried seaweed. He tells me it is gathered off the rocks, dried in the sun for a couple of hours, salted and is then ready to eat. I try some; it's OK. It has a taste reminiscent of laver bread my mam used to get me out of the fish stalls in Cardiff market. She used to fry it with bacon but that was in a more liquid form.

Just because I quite like it, it doesn't mean that I want to eat it by the bucketful but he keeps it coming. I start to wonder how long it's been in his pocket so I tell him I've had enough for now.

He tells me he's been eating it for 60 years and he's got 14 children, which is probably another good reason for not eating it. He tells me his wife eats it as well and he tells me what it does for her. I can't repeat that but you can probably work it out for yourself.

That's five days ago now and I'm still picking bits of it out of my teeth. Next day, I buy some dulse in a shop. The shopkeeper tells me that it kept thousands of people alive along that coast during the famine, so that's good.

I reckon next time I go to the pub on a Saturday night, I'll have some in my pocket and keep chewing away at it without saying anything, until they ask. By then it could be cannabis, or who-knows-what. It cost me £1.20, bet I'll get good value out of it.

If I get the village hooked on it and it has the same effect, like 14 children per family, it will help keep the village school open.

* * *

IT'S BEEN dry now for several days and I'm on my way, on the tractor, for my first full day of field work. It is logical that the driest field will be the highest field and that's where I'm headed.

In the hedgerow is one of those concrete Ordnance Survey markers that tells me I am working at 984 feet. If anyone asks, I'm working at 1,000 feet, which doesn't seem an unreasonable exaggeration in the circumstances. The only company I have up here are a neighbour's sheep in the next field and, of course, the wildlife. On the way up here, on the track that runs through the field, cock pheasants stood like sentinels every 50 yards or so.

The approaching tractor drives some of them in front of me

so they come up against their neighbours and a fight breaks out. They are so preoccupied with the fight they will break up only when the tractor is inches away and they usually take to flight, and I often wonder if they ever get their places back.

Today's job is rolling, which isn't too taxing on the concentration as long as you get the steering right. As the steering part of the job becomes instinctive you have the opportunity to switch off a bit, listen to the radio and take in your surroundings. I've been given our 'best' tractor today, which came as a bit of a surprise, and my preferred choice is Radio 2 until 5pm and then Radio 4.

About the only thing that can go wrong from a tractor-driving point of view is for the roller to become detached from the tractor. You should become quickly aware of this because the progress of the roller is marked by a sort of trundling noise you can hear even in your sound-insulated cab and above the radio.

I once had a lad working for me, who I sent rolling, who must have 'switched off' in quite a big way because he hadn't secured the metal pin that attaches roller to tractor properly. The pin had come out but he'd carried on driving for about half an hour, up and down the field, the roller sitting in splendid isolation where he'd left it.

He didn't realise what had happened until I went to see how he was getting on. He begged me not to tell anyone but refused to tell me what he was thinking about to be thus distracted. I only told one or two people: that's all you need; a story like that will soon gather its own momentum.

I turn the radio down a bit, and watch the wildlife. There are eight carrion crows busy about the field; for them it is the approach of harvest time as they busy themselves with their pillage of eggs and fledglings. I have a loathing of carrion crows that borders on hatred. I know they are doing only what is natural for them, that we've all got to live, but why do there have to be so many of them?

I try to bring a balance to all my thinking and I'm very conscious that I could be doing as much damage as them, with my roller. Apart from the cock pheasant and carrion crows, the next most numerous bird in this field is the skylark, which is good, very good.

I'm worried that the roller will damage their eggs but I watch the carrion crows carefully as they waddle about and I have not yet detected the triumphant sort of swoop that they make when they find some food; hopefully the skylarks haven't laid yet.

In the next field I have 20 acres of stubble that was left for ground-nesting birds last year and this year; it is in what we call 'set aside'. It's grown an abundance of weed plants during its first fallow year; there's plenty of food and cover there for ground-nesting birds, and I can see just as many skylarks in that field as this, so that's good as well. I've not yet seen any lapwings about, which would be even better. I try to count the pairs of skylarks in this field but it's almost impossible and I give up.

I haven't seen a hare yet, which is a concern; the grass is about nine inches tall and perfect cover. Then in the next 10 minutes I disturb three. Having exhausted my studies of the wildlife I turn my attention to the wider vista. About two miles away I can see the hills where the track of Offa's Dyke runs. Closer at hand, but a bit higher, are the sites of two Iron Age forts. They must have lived in very scary times to choose to live up there.

My mind starts to wander a bit and I think of the book I was reading last night. I have a book on the go all the time; if I haven't a new one, I will scour my shelves for an old one.

One that comes out at least once a year is Dylan Thomas' *Under Milk Wood*. Last night I was reading about the postman and his kitchen full of simmering kettles, all ready to steam open the letters. We used to have a postman around here who was a bit on the inquisitive side. As he would hand you the post he would make comments that were a giveaway: 'Joneses have had the cheque for the lambs they sold last Friday, but yours hasn't come yet.

'You're the only farmer around here who filled in the ministry census forms on time. All the others have had a reminder.' We always reckoned he used to read the holiday postcards. 'I thought Davies was going to Blackpool for a holiday but he's gone on up to the Lake District.'

One year I put him to the test and sent a neighbour a postcard from my holiday. All I wrote on it was: 'I thought Tom would like this picture.' When Tom handed my neighbour the post he said quite crossly: 'You can tell that Roger Evans I don't read the postcards.' Job done!

* * *

I HAD occasion to travel north of Shrewsbury last week. I had made a similar journey just a few days previously. On that occasion, the River Severn had been in full flood.

A torrent marked the course of the river; adjacent fields were all flooded. A glance off the bridge as I passed by last week revealed that the Severn was still swollen but quickly returning to normal levels. Signs of where the flood had been were very obvious. There, in the middle of a large field of winter wheat, 'parked up' in splendid isolation, was quite a large tree, uprooted from who knows where, floated down the river and left in the field when the waters receded.

But it was the banks of the river itself that caught my eye in particular. There, clearly marking the height that the river had reached were all the indicators of modern society. Plastic litter in a huge abundance, tons of it. What an eyesore, how sad, how long will it be there? It must be something in our national psyche that makes the dropping of litter somehow acceptable.

Yesterday, as I drove along our road, in 200 yards I passed two empty sandwich containers, two polystyrene containers that had probably contained chips, two plastic drink bottles and then, to finish, two paper napkins. It marked the clear sequence of two people's meals as they drove along, and then the sequence with which they had thrown the debris from the car.

★ ★ ★

THIS STORY has a sadness to it. I haven't kept sheep for several years now but still have a 'shepherd's eye', which I run over my neighbour's sheep (or anyone else's) as I pass by on my daily travels.

I've had some of my heifers over-wintered at a farm a couple of miles away and on one of my recent visits to see the heifers I was surprised to see them preparing a lambing pen.

I was surprised because they keep about 200 Beulah ewes – a hardy ewe, excellent mothers – and in the first week of April I had thought they would have been well able to look after themselves lambing outside.

I just love the word Beulah, it's a beautiful word, I could almost write a novel just so I could include it in the last line, 'and behold, they came over the hills and into Beulah'.

That was what they call a digression, almost a biblical type of digression. Beulah is a village in mid-Wales. Beulah ewes fill the fields for miles around, easily identifiable with their black and white, speckled faces. I expressed my surprise to those preparing the lambing pen, but to them lambing outside wasn't an option – because of the ravens.

Ravens are quite difficult to distinguish from carrion crows apart from being bigger and having a very different call.

As you know, I concern myself with the need for balance. Years ago, ravens would have been comparatively rare. The damage they would do to livestock would be occasional and not a big issue. Quite clearly the balance in this area has swung the other way and as I was finding out at first hand, it is starting to affect the way that people can farm. It is not uncommon for ewes to suffer a prolapse at lambing. Too much straining, lambs lying in the wrong position, and the odd ewe will eject her uterus. A skilled shepherd or the vet will soon put this right, administer some antibiotic and the ewe will fully recover.

In the trailer behind the quad-bike, parked alongside the lambing shed in question was a dead ewe; she had suffered a prolapse that morning, the ravens had eaten it away and she bled to death.

Lambs born outside are particularly vulnerable. While the ewe is down lambing, eyes are quickly removed from a lamb only half born. If the ewe has to leave the lamb unattended for a few minutes while she gives birth to a second, the first lamb will soon be dead because it would be attacked by the ravens. It's a sorry tale, one that I thought of quite a lot that day.

In early evening, taking a drive around, I met another neighbour who keeps sheep, driving down the lane towards me.

People who keep a lot of sheep have to be approached with caution at this time of year; they've usually got their eyes held open with matchsticks.

I pulled on to the grass verge in case he hadn't seen me, but he had, and he stopped. I told him about the ravens on the other farm and asked if he was affected. He told me that every year he has his ewes scanned to find out how many lambs a pregnant ewe is carrying. It was, therefore, his practice to lamb those ewes carrying a single lamb outside where they were able to tend to it properly and the ewes carrying two or more lambs would lamb inside where he could help them if it were needed.

Last year, several of the 'single' lambs had lost eyes to ravens but, what had particularly upset him, 20 lost their tongues while being born. These had to be put down as they were unable to suckle. This begs the question, why are there so many ravens about?

Local opinion is that they have proliferated because of the advent, locally, of large commercial shoots. These shoots provide an ample year-round supply of food; animal and vegetable. More food, more eggs, bigger hatches, fewer deaths, more ravens.

* * *

DRIVING HOME last night I saw a tiny baby rabbit on the road. It's the first one I've seen this year but I've been looking out for them because you may remember that I had noted a lot of rabbit activity just a few weeks ago. It's just another positive sign of the approach of spring.

There is another sign, actually less welcome. Around our yard there are fornicating cats everywhere. It's a part of the dilemma of feral cats about a farmyard. Ignore them, don't feed them, and they are a sickly emaciated bunch of cats that give you cause for concern. But feed them regularly, as I do, and you have a group of fit, glossy-coated cats that will breed lots and lots of kittens that will just compound the problem. Cat flu will eventually appear among the kittens, which will be a distressing sight.

I should qualify all this by saying that although I feed them all every day, there isn't one cat that we can get closer to than a couple of yards.

The answer is to have them all spayed, or neutered, and a few years ago I did try this. I caught about 20 and took them to the vet. Some escaped while there and we had cats everywhere, over the furniture, under the furniture, climbing the walls, swinging from the lights. When we finally caught them all, the vet said: 'Don't you ever bring any more like that here again.'

It's not the simple, one-off fix that people would have you

believe. New cats, male and female, turn up here quite regularly, so the problem will always be there. In the meantime we have to endure all the caterwauling and all the spitting and fighting.

★ ★ ★

YESTERDAY I saw a pheasant with 13 chicks, oh dear. Today she was in roughly the same place with 10. They seem to be very poor mothers and the approach of my tractor sends them scattering in all directions, mother leading the flight. If I was a pheasant chick I think I'd be on the phone to ChildLine to complain about the care I was receiving. There were a pair of buzzards sitting on a fence not far away and I could almost sense them licking their lips. Thirteen yesterday, 10 today, it has something about it of a rhyme I know of which is definitely not politically correct any more. Past experience tells me that she'll soon be down to one chick but that will be temporary.

★ ★ ★

ONE OF THE advantages of living in a hilly border area is superb views in all directions almost wherever we are.

I am much given to elaborating on this theme by suggesting that it isn't worth having a tidy garden because anyone visiting our garden tends to look at the views. This well-worn argument carries little credibility with my wife, who is self-appointed head gardener.

Over the years, we have settled into an uneasy truce whereby I am responsible for cutting the grass and she tends the flower beds. It's a bit like all truces, it can break down at any time. So, inevitably, we reach the time of year when I have to make a start on my lawn-mowing duties.

The lawn has, over the winter, acquired a bedraggled, unkempt look and seems to be looking at me and asking an unspoken question: 'When are you going to cut me?'

For my part, I turn my attention to the lawnmower, and look at that as well. It has become inevitable in my life that, come the day I need it for the first time, the lawnmower will not start.

It is a phenomenon that has caused many a breakdown of the aforementioned truce, because, believe it or not, it can take two weeks to start a reluctant lawnmower and we all know how much a lawn will grow in two weeks in the spring.

The two weeks is readily explained. You take the mower to your local dealer and tell him that it won't start.

But do they reach for a spanner? No they do not, they reach for a label, they write your name on it, tie it to the mower, and push it around the back where it joins a queue of other reluctant lawn mowers that is already as long as the queue at a fish and chip shop on a Friday night.

This year was going to be different, this year I was going to take the mower to the dealers just after Christmas for a check up, before the queue formed.

Inevitably, that didn't happen, so here we are, mid-March, a lawn looking at me, me looking at the mower, and my wife rolling her eyes and sighing every time she looks out of the window.

I know I need a new battery, so I get that anyway. There's a conversation at the dealers between the man in the stores and the proprietor over whether the battery needs charging or not. They decide it doesn't. I take the battery home and fit it on and I fill the tank up with petrol and determine to leave it for 24 hours – this is the lawnmower equivalent of poking a stick into a squirrel's drey and telling it: 'Spring is here'.

A day later, I return, make a big, slow deal of putting all the controls in the right places, turn the key and the battery is flat as a pancake. This is the sort of setback I'm well used to, so I put the battery on charge and go away and leave it.

I almost forget all about it the next day, but it's Friday evening, the boys have nearly finished washing the parlour out. It's time for tea but I decide to try the mower. I turn the key and it bursts into life first turn. This completely throws me. I sit there for a minute and it doesn't stop. I'm now in shock – still, make hay while the sun shines, etc, and off I go, there's nearly an hour of daylight yet and I cut most of the lawns. I leave the worst piece for another day.

If I am thrown, pity my wife. She can't believe what's happened – never had the grass cut so soon. Next day I tell her I will take her out for supper if Wales win the Triple Crown. Cut grass, an unexpected meal – she thinks I'm having an affair.

***

ABOUT EIGHT years ago a farmer at a show told me how he had gone to market in a brand new Land Rover, bought some cattle and duly backed his trailer up to the loading pens.

At market there are gates to put in place for loading and he'd dropped the ramp of his trailer and gone to get the cattle, putting various gates in place as he went. It is then a simple task to drive the cattle back to the trailer.

The first cattle went on to the trailer ramp and the trailer sat up in the air because in the few minutes he had been away (and never out of sight) someone had taken the Land Rover.

The worst bit was still to come; his insurance company wouldn't pay out a penny because he had left the keys in the Land Rover.

At that time, we as a family never took a key out of any vehicle, day or night. I went home that night and established a new regime whereby all keys had to be taken out at all times.

At first it was a damn nuisance – so many time I walked up to the yard, got in the car and then had to go back in the house for the keys.

There was another new regime established here last night. I locked the kitchen door when I went to bed. It felt really strange; I would guess that it's the first time the door has been locked in 45 years. In fact, we had no idea where the key was and had to buy a new lock just to get a key!

Last week my wife had some money stolen out of the drawer in the kitchen. It's money she puts by for Christmas. If I'd known it was there I could have warned her someone would steal it – I'd have had some myself.

It's left a really strange collection of feelings, the worst of which is the sort of witch-hunt that goes on in your mind as you search for culprits.

It's not fair on us and it's not fair on the people who work here. It was too much money not to involve the police, not that I think they will find anyone – there was little enough for them to work on and no forced entry.

What is a shame is that it has changed the way we live our lives. The shed where we keep all our tools is wide open and that's next on our list of 'to dos'.

Strangely, when we came to live here over 40 years ago, every shed, loose box, granary and cattle yard was locked every night with a padlock and the farm foreman had to take this huge bunch of keys to the house every night when he finished work.

The reason for that would almost certainly have been the fact that they were only just coming out of an era when farm workers lived (only just) on subsistence wages.

Most of them would have poultry, or if they were the lucky ones, they would have had a pig. There would be hardly any waste food in their lives and the bosses' grain stores would be very attractive.

The place where the corn grinder was kept was built with 2in-thick boards and was as impenetrable as Fort Knox.

Life always goes in cycles, and here we are locking things up again. It makes me a bit sad.

* * *

WE HAVE three fields of maize this year, which is more than usual. One of the fields should have gone into winter wheat last autumn but the ground was too wet to do a tidy job of working and sowing, so we decided it was better to leave it.

With modern kit and powerful four-wheel drive tractors it is possible to sow a crop into soil conditions that you just would not have contemplated years ago. But if the soil is not right you will see the results come spring, with lots of bare patches where the crop has simply not grown.

Two of our maize crops were sown by 7 May, which is the date I always have in my mind as a deadline. We're in borderline maize-growing country here because of our height above sea level and if we sow it any earlier, it can suffer damage from late frosts.

Our worst growing years are hot, dry ones, because we have a low depth of soil and the grass will die off (we call it burning). Maize will thrive in those conditions and keep on growing and bulk up.

You can concentrate on producing top quality forage as much as you like but if you run out of forage at the end of January you are, to put it mildly, in a bit of a mess. Maize is a good banker for a dry year.

Our third field of maize was sown about 10 days later. This was because it was being planted into a grass field from which we wanted to firstly take some silage.

So we took a crop of grass and then there followed a frantic week, spreading manure, ploughing and working it down and, of course, drilling the maize.

We have a good young lad who works here part time but he also has his own tractor and he soon gets tempted away to join silage gangs for large contractors, so the week turned out to be more frantic than we thought.

Anyway, the maize went in in good order and because it was later going in we drilled it at a lower seed rate, 40,000 an acre, so that the plants mature a bit quicker in the slightly shorter time they will have.

The dog and I, driving past the field a couple of days later, reckoned between us that there were 200-300 rooks on there. This might have been OK but then again, it might not. There was a fair chance they were eating grubs, which was good. But while they stab away in the soil looking for grubs they could turn up a bright yellow thing and think: 'Look everybody, corn on the cob.'

The dog, who is a lot brighter than me, reckoned that 250 rooks eating 10 seeds a day for a week would make a fair inroad into the 40,000 we drilled.

I reckoned it was much worse than that because they cart a lot more than that back to their nests.

Clearly, we needed to monitor the situation closely. It can, if you let it, drive you to distraction. They would be there just after 4am until late at night. I could get up early and fire a shotgun at them but I doubt if I'd ever hit one; it would just make me feel better.

My neighbours, on the other hand, wouldn't like it at all. Nor would they like bird-scarer guns going all day.

There had to be a better way. A quick phone call to the keeper and within an hour he had shot one rook and examined the contents of its crop, which was full of grubs, so I had nothing to worry about.

He said he would shoot another in three or four days time to see if their diet had changed. But in three or four days time there wasn't a rook to be seen and the maize was coming up fine.

Summer

WE'VE BEEN doing our silage these last two days. It's a contractor who does the work, and he can clear 60 or 70 acres a day if everything goes OK. He has a huge machine that picks the crop up, chops it up and blows it into trailers. Today, there are four tractors and trailers carting the cut grass and they are struggling to keep him going. It's a bit 'rip and tear', or would 'frenetic' be a better way to describe it?

Our farm adjoins a B-road, and where you join it as you come out of our farm, it is not that easy to see oncoming traffic. We have a couple of young lads driving tractors so I thought a bit of safety wouldn't go amiss. I bought two big red triangles with pictures of tractors in the middle and I nailed these signs on to pallets. I put one either side of the junction, giving about 100 yards warning of the hazard. I thought I was doing something that would make young lives safer. I didn't realise my own would be at risk. You'd think someone carrying a pallet across the road with a big red triangle fixed to it would attract attention. I was glad to get back into the Discovery. I certainly wasn't safe putting the signs up. So I've done my bit. Does anyone pay any attention?

Not that I've seen. If it wasn't so serious, it would almost be funny. Going to work in the morning is the most dangerous time, with builders in vans, late for work and eating bacon sandwiches, and women doing 70mph while they put their make-up on.

* * *

IT CAN be very exciting, going on holiday, but I always look forward to the first ride around the farm when I get back. I like to look at the stock and the fields and mentally note the changes that have taken place. I set off this morning also quite excited, which may seem a bit sad but to me it means that I find my everyday life fulfilling. I was looking particularly to see some improvement in the maize, and there was. The weedkiller has worked well and the plants have grown — a bit. I don't know how many times I was told in France that the French maize looks better than mine — and it did.

* * *

THERE'S A LANE I travel every day to get to our other land. A kestrel lives somewhere near the lane, he or she has been there for years. I tend to drive along the lane slowly as I look over the hedges (being nosey) and the kestrel has taken to flying along in front of whatever vehicle, tractor or Discovery that I'm driving. At this time of year, the sound of an approaching vehicle can make fledglings cross the road from one hedgerow to the other. We don't have to travel very far, the kestrel and I, before he has a meal. It leaves me feeling as if I were being used, which of course I am.

Through the window about 100 yards away is a small clump of trees I planted years ago in a wet place below our pond. There were two pairs of carrion crows there this morning kicking up a noise. I always think the word 'alight' is very descriptive. When you say a bird alights it creates a vision of a bird landing gently on a bough. It doesn't describe in any way what these carrion crows are up to this morning. They are working the clump of trees methodically to flush out game and when they see the game they crash into the branches and bushes with force. Their behaviour tells me that there are some fledglings about that have just left the nest and they are hunting them down. I don't know what species they are chasing but I see all this going on and it really annoys me.

I'd like to put some lead shot into them but they'd be long gone before I got into range, they'd watch me from a safe distance and return to their slaughter as soon as I disappeared. By lunchtime they will have done their worst and moved on somewhere else. Some people blame farmers for the decline in songbirds, when all about me I see birds of prey and other predators wrecking havoc with bird populations.

At this time of year our dry cows, cows that are resting between one spell of giving milk and the arrival of their next calf, are all away on our other land and it is important to check them closely every day. I need to see if they are approaching calving and that their udders are healthy. A modern dairy cow's life is a busy one and this eight to 10 week period of rest and relaxation is an important time. We check their feet before they go away and trim them if necessary; a few weeks off concrete, recharging their batteries, works wonders. My holidays seem to do the opposite for me but then my dry cows don't stay up too late and drink too much wine.

Earlier this morning, I saw a hare and a pheasant sitting in the maize. I see hares and pheasants in the maize every day, so what's different about these two? Well, they were both sitting close together. If the pheasant's wing had been an arm it could have put it around the hare. I watched them for five minutes before

I moved on and they were still there. What do you reckon was going on?

* * *

IT'S MORE than a month now since I went around the landlord's 6m margins with the topper. There is supposed to be a 2m strip cut into these margins on the side nearest the field.

It was once explained to me that these were for birds to dry off after heavy rain. If that is true, then the strips will have come into their own this year.

What particularly caught my eye was how much these margins have changed in their nature and composition in the three or four years they have been there.

I was also told that the idea of the margins was to provide wildlife corridors around fields. When we first left them they were obviously also a valuable food source because what was left to grow was the remnants of what was there before, be it grassland or cereals.

These would obviously go to seed and provide a good food source for birds in the winter. But the nature of these margins is changing with time.

Most of the food sources have now disappeared and boar thistles and ragwort catch my eye. This last year, I have noted that the beginnings of trees are appearing, especially blackthorn and saplings, that look a bit like willow but obviously aren't.

Given a few more years, I don't think these margins will be doing what they are supposed to. I was always told that they were RSPB-inspired, and you have to ask yourself if these people who seek to take over the countryside actually know what they are doing. In a few years' time I will probably report that we have had to take a chainsaw to the margins so that wildlife can get through.

TODAY I'm topping a field, cutting off grass that has given way to seed, of which there's a fair bit, but mostly where dung pats have been deposited thus far in the grazing season.

There are a few thistles and lots and lots of docks. I like to hear docks going through the topper so there are lots of nice noises coming from behind me.

There are quite a few plants that I call burdocks – I'm not really sure if that's the right name. It's a plant that grows a sort of burr that clings to your clothes. They have a tough woody stem and go through the topper with a clunk.

I decide that the docks have gone beyond what is acceptable and therefore decide, as I drive along, that I will spray them when they regrow.

There's quite a lot of white clover in this field and that will disappear with the spray, but I can put some clover back into it – it's better to lose the docks.

Cock pheasants are at the skulking stage of their annual cycle and when I start the process of topping there's not one to be seen but as I progress with my work, one by one they come out of the undergrowth and when I go to the gate, job finished, I look back and count 20 cocks in the field.

The hens I've disturbed can't be seen and so far this year I've not seen a pheasant hen with chicks.

I ponder on the subject of burdocks. There used to be a soft drink available in my childhood called dandelion and burdock – a sort of coke-coloured drink – but just which part of either plant was used to make it, I have no idea.

* * *

LAST WEEK saw the last ever Royal Show at Stoneleigh. If someone had told me that 20 years ago I would never have believed them. In the past we always went in a car-load, going early and coming back late.

We would rest on large stands provided by the banks, who would offer a gin and tonic without even asking if you were a client.

There would be countless stands selling wine and farmers who looked a bit affluent would be encouraged to try a few samples.

I can't remember being asked to try some, which is a stigma that still hurts today. There would be a pig unit there, a dairy unit and, if I remember correctly, a poultry unit, too. One by one these units, like the attendees, have drifted away.

Our milk co-operative used to have a stand there and I would be on duty for four days but it's an expensive business and every year we would see fewer and fewer members.

The last time we were there was particularly hot and there was a nice lot of skin to be seen.

As times in general have become tougher, people in agriculture have tended to identify with the major shows in their locality, like the Bath and West and Cornwall, and that great success story, the Royal Welsh.

The Royal at Stoneleigh was 'everyone's' show, but not sadly, anymore. At this year's I received a fellowship of the Royal Agriculture Society of England, which was a proud day for me.

I've been an associate for a few years now so I've moved from a sort of lance corporal up to sergeant.

Honours don't fall on dairy farmers very often. What usually falls on dairy farmers comes from under a cow's tail.

* * *

A COUPLE of years ago we were given a barn owl nesting box. It's never been out in place, just moved around as we have gone through tidying up processes.

It has been a doll's house, a garage, a kitten's cottage, but an owl it has never seen. We have given it some thought – we've tried to identify where it would most likely be used.

There's things like height and safety to consider and we're not big on height here.

But there is a barn owl regularly working one of our bottom fields and there is a big old oak tree in the middle of the field, so it seems obvious, at last, where to put it.

Barn owls are just about as beautiful as creatures get. They are probably benefitting from the 6m margins around fields and the extra hunting areas that this provides. Good luck to them.

★ ★ ★

WE WENT out with friends for a meal on Saturday evening to the pub in a village not far from here. It's quite an unusual pub because like a lot of pubs in small villages, it has struggled from time to time, so it was bought by the community some years ago and, despite one or two ups and downs, it is flourishing at the moment.

Later in the evening while sitting by the window in my observation mode, I saw an old Discovery come down the road and turn into the car park.

Some time ago I watched a TV programme where they showed how to fly a Jumbo jet from New York to Heathrow entirely by computer. So accurate was this that when the plane landed at Heathrow it straddled exactly the white line down the runway. The Discovery came down the road like the plane, straddling the white line.

The driver came in after a while. He used to be a local agricultural contractor; someone in our group said he's 90 next month.

Two years ago I saw him at a ploughing match doing a fair job with his vintage tractor and two-furrow plough. Everyone knows him; he's lived in the village all his life.

He got himself a pint and retired to a quiet corner, obviously contented and at ease. He got out the paraphernalia that he needed to roll himself a cigarette and did it quickly and expertly. Then, sadly for me, he had to go outside to smoke it.

He's probably been drinking in the pub since he was 10, and when he first drove down the main road there probably weren't any white lines on it.

I've never smoked and I think pubs are the better for the ban but I somehow feel he's earned the right, at his age, to smoke his roll-up where he likes.

When we left he'd just finished it and we had a five-minute chat. It was a beautiful warm evening and he seemed unconcerned about having to move with the times, something he's obviously always taken in his stride.

* * *

WE'VE got a really good lad who works here part-time. He comes three days a week in the winter and when he can in the summer.

Summer is his busy time because he's bought his own tractor and goes off doing contract work – all very enterprising in a lad who is only just 17. I wouldn't want him to know I think he's a good lad because it's also important to keep him on his toes as he spends a lot of time trying to keep me on mine.

His social life is of interest to me and I'm always surprised by how many fights there are at the dances he attends. I see it as my role to teach him a bit of homespun philosophy and to avoid these fights and to concentrate on the girls instead.

'This,' I told him, pointing to my head, 'is for thinking, and these,' pointing to my feet, 'are for dancing and running away.'

He's not been here for some weeks now – last time he was here he was carting muck on to our maize ground. There was a huge heap outside a shed that we clean out every month during the winter. He wanted a couple of hours off at noon to go for a driving lesson so I said I'd clear out the remaining muck in the shed while he was away.

'Take you a lot longer than two hours to do that,' he said. 'It's all very well you young boys ripping and tearing about on these machines and making a lot of noise,' I told him, 'but now and again someone like me has to take a hand. My superior tractor driving skills, knowledge and expertise are needed to keep work up to schedule and, if you are bright enough, it gives you a chance to learn from the high standards I set.'

He thought this was all very funny and went off to his lesson saying: 'You won't clear that shed out before I get back!'

I leant nonchalantly on a gate until he was out of sight but then I leapt into action. It's the best shed we have for cleaning out – in a previous life it was a large grain store, so it's got nice concrete walls and floors.

A lot of our sheds are not concreted right through because the cost of concrete in recent years has been prohibitive. In fact, it would probably be cheaper to cover the floors with the finest Indian carpets.

The previous tenant to me, who used the shed as a grain store, had lined the roof with plastic fertiliser bags. I don't know why, perhaps it was to stop condensation, but I've noticed that lots of pigeons live in the space between the bags and the roof.

The roar from the machine disturbed them and I'd got my fifth bucket full when two very young pigeons came fluttering out from their sanctuary and landed on my bucket.

I had two choices: carry on regardless and tip muck and pigeons on the heap outside; or get off, catch them and put them somewhere safe.

I chose the latter, of course, but my mind was on my young

helper – I didn't need this delay. I pressed on with my work and had to stop three or four times more to remove pigeons from the bucket, including the pigeons I'd removed to safety but which had fluttered back on to the bucket.

The shed was clear, the loader parked up and I was back leaning on the gate before the world's best tractor driver got back. He popped his head inside the shed door and, to be fair, gave me a congratulatory nod. Now here's a strange thing. As I got off the loader while dealing with the pigeons I muttered 'bloody quist' to myself.

I don't know how you spell it but you pronounce it *kwist*. It's a word I'd not used for years and years but have used before to describe a pigeon.

I left the lad to his work and went off thinking about my automatic use of the word 'quist'. I lived the first 20 years of my life in Monmouthshire and wondered if it was a word that came from the Welsh.

I phoned a Welsh-speaking friend that night but he'd never heard it. A friend in Monmouthshire hadn't either.

I told him another word I used to use was pronounced 'een', which described a ewe in the act of lambing. He'd heard that, saying: 'An old boy who used to work here at one time always used to say een.'

Thank you very much.

I used to employ a real star of a man, who'd be well into his 80s now. He'd been dragged off the farm where the shed and pigeons are during the war, because he was the only single employee there to join the army.

He hated his induction training so much that he volunteered for a role, not specifically described, that would earn him an extra two and sixpence a week. A couple of months later he found himself jumping out of a plane over Arnhem.

Jack always used to bring two thermos flasks to work. One contained ordinary tea and one contained tea and whisky.

At the time, I had a business that used to export game products to France and Jack and I used to drive hundreds of miles together. If ever I was to lose my licence for drinking and driving it would have been because of what was in his number two flask. But he didn't call them flasks, he called them costrils.

'Bit cold this morning,' he'd say. 'Had to give number two costril a bit extra.'

'Why do you call them costrils, Jack?'

'No idea,' he'd say, 'always called them costrils.'

Then, one day, I visited the Welsh Folk museum at St Fagan's on the west of Cardiff – very well worth a visit.

There, hanging on chains under a hay wagon, was a tiny barrel that would have been used to take cider to the hay field. It's name? A costril.

* * *

OVER the last few months, new signs have been appearing in the area denoting a national cycle path.

The chap who works for us cycles half a mile to and from work and I thought at first it was to show him how to get to his house, but it's obviously a lot more than that.

By strange coincidence, the signs follow exactly the route that was historically taken from London to Aberystwyth. This was a very direct route taking straight lines across country whenever possible. I always thought it was originally planned on a map that didn't possess contour lines, because it is up and down some very hard pulls.

I used to think: poor bloody horses. I don't extend that concern to the cyclists because they have more choice than the horses ever had.

There was time when I did a lot of cycling to keep fit and sometimes I am minded to take it up again, as a recreation. A friend once told me that a lot of disused railway lines are now cycle paths and railway lines rarely go up steep hills – that seems an eminently more sensible option.

He once told me he had cycled from Merthyr to the centre of Cardiff and went home on the train – a ride almost entirely downhill. Excellent.

★ ★ ★

IF EVER you come to our house, and you are very welcome – bed and breakfast, en suite, reasonable rates – you will discover that our back yard slopes down to our house, that there are buildings on two sides of the slope and the house is at the bottom.

If I tidied our kitchen table up and let you in, you would also discover that it is a typically large farmhouse kitchen, and that you need to go down three steps from the kitchen to the rest of the house.

Earlier this week we had the mother and father of all thunderstorms. I was putting a machine on a tractor to go thistle cutting and took shelter in an adjacent building.

It was raining so hard it was quite spectacular but after a quarter of an hour, I decided I would be as well off in the house and do a bit of writing.

I didn't have a coat with me so the 50-yard dash would have soaked me to the skin but the Discovery was sheltering in the shed with me, so I took that to get to the house.

I'd never seen so much water going down the back yard and you could see that although the drain wasn't blocked, it just couldn't cope and the water was rising at the kitchen door.

There was already an inch of water in the kitchen when I opened the door. I've always thought of myself as resourceful, so I went straight to the airing cupboard and got out some blankets.

I put one against the door that leads to our living room, where the water was now starting to accumulate, one at the top of the steps to stop the waterfall that was gathering pace and then tried to brush some water back out of the door.

This was a complete waste of time so I put the third blanket across the bottom of the door and with two feet and the broom head, managed to keep it in place and stood there for half an hour.

I did open the door a fraction to see what was happening but the water was six inches above the doorstep. Eventually the storm abated and I was able to clear what was now three inches of water back out through the door. It took me two hours of sweeping and mopping to restore order.

My wife was out during this drama and when she returned home the kitchen was fairly clean, I had lit the Rayburn to speed up the drying process (always a plus where my wife is concerned). Most important of all, I had stopped the deluge flooding the rest of the house.

A few years ago we had a similar experience but there were no heroes on hand to save the day. Our living/dining room was flooded. We worked hard shampooing the carpet and hired dehumidifiers and thought we'd done a good job but three days later the carpet started to stink.

If ever you see flood victims on television waiting for new carpets and fittings, don't be tempted to think they are trying it on because the filth and smell left by a flood is appalling.

Personally, my own heroic efforts went largely unheralded and I felt a bit like the little Dutch boy who saved the community by putting his finger in the dyke, but without the recognition.

My next-door neighbour, who knows everything, and certainly more than is good for him, reckons we had an inch and a quarter of rain in 40 minutes, most of which came down our back yard.

* * *

ON A never-to-be-forgotten Sunday a couple of weeks ago I caught two moles, one an hour after I laid the trap. One was still alive; the trap had caught him by his leg. I had some difficulty deciding what to do with him.

You have to have some admiration for these little animals and how they live their lives; I just wish they would do it somewhere else. I don't mind trapping them and killing them, I just prefer it to be out of sight down the burrow.

I told my daughter I'd put it in a bucket of water. 'That won't do, moles are good swimmers,' she said. Not with a mole trap on their leg, they're not.

* * *

OUTSIDE it's cold, very wet and very miserable. The livestock are miserable and all the staff are miserable. It wouldn't be a particularly bad day in the middle of February but we're at the start of June. It's a good day to sneak into the house to write but only because the Rayburn is keeping the kitchen cosy.

Earlier today I was reminiscing. I've reached the stage of my life when my wife says that I have more to remember than I have to look forward to, but I have one or two things up my sleeve I haven't told her about yet.

A week ago we went to a promise auction for the village school and that's what started me off on my reminiscing. I used to be very involved at the school, chair of governors, chair of PTA, unofficial lifeguard at their weekly swimming lessons, but children grow up and your life moves on.

Yet here we were again in the village hall at a social event on a Saturday evening to raise money for the school. Our attendance was at the request of my daughter whose daughter has just started at the school, the third generation in our family.

It reminded me how much fun you can have with rural fundraising. The first time I raised money in this area was many years ago when I organised a raffle for the rugby club. It was one of those proper Christmas raffles with an official licence and lots of prizes. Getting to the last two prizes, and also getting a little jaded, I found that someone in our local town had won a pair of tights and someone in Blackpool had won a turkey. I've always been a practical, commonsense sort of person and it seemed to me eminently sensible to swap the prizes over and send the tights to Blackpool. Someone found out what I'd done and reported me to the authorities and I got into quite serious trouble, and still ended up sending a turkey to Blackpool.

When I was chair of the PTA I used to have an annual battle with the ladies on the committee, they were all ladies on the committee except me. We used to run a dance every year in the village hall. I would insist on a local farmer doing the music. He had no lights, no effects, just a deck and some records but

he only charged £15. That meant we were into profit as soon as the committee had bought tickets. He always used to bring a spot prize with him which would be won by the couple dancing closest to a rusty nail stuck in the ceiling. He always chose the same nail, same spot, so the spot dance always became something of a rugby scrum. The year after I retired the ladies had a live band and lost £150.

A couple of years ago, we had a golf day at the rugby club and the first prize was a pig. Everyone was going ha ha, very funny, but secretly suspecting it was a frozen pig for the deep freeze. Some of them were already smacking their lips in anticipation of the crackling. Actually it wasn't a frozen pig, it was a fresh one. Very fresh, alive and well and weighing about 200lbs. They let it loose in the clubhouse where it ran amok as it rooted about for food scraps left from the dinner we'd just had. Half the people were on the floor because their chairs had been knocked over and half were on the tables because they were afraid of it.

My favourite fundraising story is of the cheese and wine we held here at the house once for the rugby club. Things got a bit out of hand, as they do, and someone fetched the children's donkey out of the field and into the house and raised a lot of money giving donkey rides — once around the kitchen and twice around the sitting room for a £1. Women with tight skirts were 50p. The donkey was impeccably behaved from a lavatorial point of view.

Our promise auction for the school was fun. If you were associated with a school in a large town or city you probably wouldn't get the chance to buy a load of manure, two tractor batteries or some hay. There was a load of logs on offer that made £70. The £70 was bid by the person who had given the logs. I had to ask why he had done it. 'What time have I got to cut a load of logs?' came the reply.

* * *

I'M OFF to bed, as usual, fairly early – it's where I do most of my reading. There are three of our bed and breakfast guests in their sitting room, I've not yet met them, so I pause to say hello.

They ask me for a corkscrew to open a bottle of wine, which I get, along with three better wine glasses than the ones they are using.

They ask me to join them in a drink, which I decline, but I do sit down for a chat. The conversation drifts towards wildlife. They have been watching our pond and, in particular, the mallard and her young, and a coot and her young. The mallard ducklings are declining in number and I suspect the coots are to blame.

I tell them I've been watching *Springwatch*. They tell me they love the programme, but just can't put up with Bill Oddie, so they don't watch it any more.

I can sympathise with that, perhaps it's because dairy farmers are more used to adversity and become more pragmatic, but I tolerate Bill Oddie because I enjoy seeing the wildlife.

It's a classic case of a 'celebrity' who thinks his ego is more important than the programme. On one show he talked about a species of bird being reintroduced to the UK. The reintroduction was set back a year when the birds strayed off their sanctuary on to a farm where they were 'inevitably' poisoned. He was saying quite clearly that farms are synonymous with a poisoned environment. How disgraceful is that?

He wants squeezing into a wetsuit and dropping in a cold loch, where, with a bit of luck, he might be picked up by an osprey and fed to its young – all shown on camera, of course.

We move our own conversation on, thankfully, and it gets a bit competitive with, 'Have you seen this?' and 'Have you ever seen that?'

I can compete quite well until they tell me they have often seen otters. I'm quite envious, I've never seen an otter in the wild

– lots of people who spend their lives in the countryside never do. It's often down to chance, right place, right time sort of stuff. My son David was coming to work once and found two dead on the road, which was a real shame.

My bed and my book are calling and I get up to go, but they haven't quite finished. 'I tell you what we haven't seen for years and years,' one of them says. 'A brown hare.'

I turn in the doorway and reply, 'I can show you a hare.'

I arrange to collect them at the front door next morning, to take them to see a hare.

Next day I look inside my truck and decide it will take longer to make it clean than I have time to do it, so I borrow David's. Mert, my dog, has to come which is a bit of a treat for him, but he can't see as much out of the front window because there are two rows of seats in this vehicle, so he's not so pleased as he thought he would be. The first field we go in is the one we have to leave in stubble for 12 months for the ground-nesting birds. It starts off as a clean stubble but, come the spring, everything grows, be it weeds or seed from previous crops.

So now we have a waist-high jungle of wheat, barley, oilseed rape, grasses, docks, thistles and nettles. It's perfect cover for ground-nesting birds because the height of the growth is cover from aerial predators. The keeper tells me a fox has been living there for two months, which isn't quite so perfect.

I drive slowly through the field and wonder if the hares will turn up. It's getting quite hot now and they may have sought some shade.

Fifty yards away I see the grasses move suddenly and a glimpse of a brown body. The movement continues and I suspect we've found the fox. I drive up closer in to a clearer space and we find two hares fighting and playing.

I switch the engine off and they play round and round us for about five minutes. My guests are in raptures and camcorders and cameras are kept busy. It's almost like a safari where the big cats come up to the vehicles.

We and the hares move on and I drive around the fields we have recently cut for silage. The regrown grass is almost 6in tall now, about up to a reclining hare's shoulders, and we can see brown hares everywhere. We started counting them, but gave up when we reached 20.

As we continue our short journey, we meet hares coming towards us, hares running away, and hares up on their haunches, watching us watching them. Hares to the right of us, hares to the left of us.

As if on cue, all the birds turn up as well – lots of different species and, to be fair, my guests are very knowledgeable. Our journey done, we return home. It's not taken an hour, but their thanks are profuse. 'What you've just shown us is priceless,' says the woman. 'No, it isn't,' I reply, 'we charge £3 a hare and Ann will put it on your bill.'

I don't get £3 a hare, but I do get a very nice bottle of red wine.

* * *

I OFTEN fill my car up with petrol on Sunday mornings on my way to see my daughter and her children.

It doesn't seem long ago that a full tank would cost £50. Last Sunday it was £72!

This comes particularly hard for someone of a generation who, at one time, would have thought nothing of taking five gallons of red diesel down the fields to light a bonfire and if there were a couple of gallons left in the tin, throwing that on the fire as well, to save carrying it back.

THUS FAR this season we've been lucky enough to take our two silage cuts in good order, and most importantly, in good weather. Those in the neighbourhood who farm beef and sheep, work to a different timescale.

They tend to graze their grass fields in the winter and spring and take just one cut of silage and much of that is round bales.

They probably number in the majority around here, so while we are watching the hot sun and very heavy showers speed the growth of our third cut of silage, they are in the throes of what must be quite a difficult season.

Round bales wrapped in plastic were among the best things that ever happened as far as livestock are concerned. It took them from a diet that in many years was very bad hay to a palatable, nutritious feed of silage that could be made very simply in a 24-hour window.

Once it was wrapped it was safe and the bales could be carted at leisure, whatever the weather, and stacked outside to feed during the winter as required.

Even in a season like this it is possible to make good, round-bale silage. But one or two of my neighbours have still been tempted to try and make hay.

I've never made much hay in my farming career. I've never had much luck in my life, certainly not enough spare to try hay-making.

What these neighbours have been tempted to do is save the cost of the plastic wrap.

'Forecast not too bad, those showers might not affect us, we'll make hay of those two fields,' I've been told.

Now there are several fields around here that come into that category. They've been cut several days, successively soaked and dried several times, and they look brown and worthless.

My wife's late father used to be philosophical about making some bad hay. He used to keep a herd of Hereford suckler cows that were out-wintered and calved in the spring. If he had a bay or two of poor hay it was always considered good enough for the cows. Which was fair enough, but if he made all his hay perfectly he would worry about what he would give the cows, as good hay was considered too good for them! They would probably end up having to eat straw and swedes.

I could never quite get my head around that. Probably he thought that some bales of good hay would keep until the next year, when he might not get much good hay at all but plenty that was good enough for the cows.

I often used to help him feed them on Sunday mornings and wondered, as I threw wads of mouldy hay off the trailer, white with mould they would be, how the cows survived on their diet. But they did.

* * *

I ALWAYS drive slowly through the small village where my daughter lives. It's more of a hamlet, really – no shop, no pub – and the road through it doesn't go anywhere in particular, so traffic is minimal and children can play in the road and adults can stand and chat in it.

I often think that bypasses around most villages would be the making of them, taking traffic away and restoring peace and calm. I might put that in my manifesto.

On the last occasion I drove through there was a man standing in the middle of the road with his arm outstretched, so I slowed down even more.

Purposeful border collies then appeared from all directions, fully intent on their work. They popped out of this gate, over the garden wall. I hadn't seen them but I knew there were sheep about.

I recognised the collies. There were five of them and they travel with their owner everywhere in his Land Rover.

He rarely lets them all out at the same time, as he explained to me: 'Some of them like to eat sheep, some like to eat people, some like to do both.'

They are known locally to be very fierce and if ever I go to his yard I will never get out of the Discovery. They have been known to bite holes in vehicle tyres. But I let them get on with it – better a tyre than my leg and to be fair, Brian will always help you to change the wheel.

Brian came down the village in his Land Rover, looking hot and flustered. He got out and told the man in the road that it was OK, the sheep had forced their way through the fence in so-and-so's garden.

He came to speak to me, too: 'It took us over an hour to bring these sheep half-a-mile to dip them. They're in the pen now but I think I'll get them back out, they've been in everyone's garden except one so they might as well go in there while we're at it.' And off he went to his dipping.

It is a huge problem moving stock if they have to go through a village. Forty years ago, village gardens would be stock-proof because villagers would know that from time to time stock would be on the road, either on purpose or strayed. These days it never occurs to them.

Brian would have had 300–400 sheep in this particular group and it would be a huge job to transfer them from field to dipping pen in a lorry or trailer. The sheep themselves would much prefer the short dash down the road, especially if it includes nipping around a few gardens on the way.

It's years and years since we kept sheep but their grazing land was on one side of the village and we live on the other and we ended up taking the sheep through the village several times a year. In some ways sheep are worse than cattle, because with cattle I can put lengths of bale string in appropriate places and the cattle, thinking it to be electric fence, stay on the straight and narrow, usually.

One day we were moving the sheep, probably 300 ewes, plus their lambs, and once they were started on their journey, I went on in front in the van to shut what garden gates there still were in the village. I was getting on quite well and was just shutting one gate when a voice accosted me: 'What the hell do you think you are doing?'

'I'm shutting your garden gate.'

'I don't want my garden gate shut.'

'But the sheep are coming, I'll open it afterwards.'

'Leave my gate alone.'

And he stalked back into the house.

Never liked the man, really: ex-army, newcomer, thought he owned the whole village, sang in the church choir so he thought he was the vicar as well.

My daughter has solemnly promised me that she won't allow him to sing in the choir at my funeral, she being in charge of all arrangements.

There's always been an unfortunate side to my character that can't resist situations like this. We had at the time a most remarkable bearded collie working dog. She was without doubt the cleverest dog I have ever had. Mert's quite clever but if they'd been at school he would have been in the D stream and she in the A.

I waited for the sheep to arrive and stood on the opposite side of the road to the open garden gate. Poppy (terrible name, good dog) came to me when she saw me on the footpath.

She was clever; she always seemed to know what I wanted. None of this 'come by' and 'away by' - just a click of the tongue or a bit of a whistle.

I waited until the sheep were half past the garden gate and gave a click and she was away in front of the sheep, her in front and the boys pushing at the back. Well, there was only one place for them to go, and go they did. A couple of laps of honour round the garden and back out.

He wasn't best pleased and tried to claim on my insurance but couldn't build a case because I'd taken all reasonable care. Bit of a bugger, really.

* * *

MY SON-IN-LAW has put me on standby to drive his combine for two days at the end of the week. Whether I actually get to drive it depends entirely on the weather.

I've never had a combine, never grown enough corn to need one, but I have on occasion driven for other people in similar circumstances.

My son-in-law's combine is fairly old and relatively small by modern standards but it is pristine in condition and when you are up there driving it you do feel just a bit important.

It's a strange phenomenon but when you do drive someone

else's combine, parts of it become yours. For example, if a bearing should go while you are driving it, no one says 'a bearing has just gone', they say 'Roger broke a bearing'.

Never mind that the bearing might be 20 years old, never mind that all you've actually done is put the mechanism into gear and made the bearing go round, which it's supposed to do anyway.

And if the same bearing should seize up in five years' time, they'll say: 'Roger broke that bearing a few years ago and it's never been the same since.'

So while you are driving along, all nonchalant, you are listening for anything that sounds a bit different because you know that the name of the part that breaks and your name will be linked together forever.

This linking of names and parts will be relatively local. It will start off in the pub where the farmers are comparing notes after a day's harvesting.

'How did you get on today?'

'OK. But we lost two hours when Roger broke that long shaft that goes down from the drum to the whatsit.'

But that story will only go around two or three other pubs and will soon run out of momentum because as sure as night follows day, someone else will break something much more interesting.

There is an ultimate sin to combine driving. When you transfer the grain from the combine to the trailer there's a big auger that sticks out at the side, a bit like a phallic symbol, that unloads the grain. This folds back into the combine when not in use. You should never forget to fold it back when unloading is done because if you forget it is still sticking out, you are likely to wrap it around a tree and if you do that, the story will travel from pub to pub and from parish to parish.

A useful tip for would-be combine drivers, if something breaks, is always look hopeless and helpless with a spanner in your hand. If you get too involved you get covered in oil and grease and all the bits of chaff and straw that stick to it. Wouldn't want that, would we? It's far better for someone else to do all that.

* * *

ONE OF the most important parts of my role within our dairy co-operative is communicating with our members. Members own the co-operative, they *are* the co-operative, their milk is the lifeblood of the co-operative and without their milk, there is no co-operative.

There are all sorts of ways of communicating and one of the most important is on a one-to-one basis at stands at agricultural shows. There are about 2,500 members in total and I expect I've spoken to most of them.

When I go to a show like the Royal Welsh, for example, I spend four days talking to people and the only bit of the show I see is between our stand and the toilets.

On the first day a member I know well was sitting down opposite me with his wife. From past experience, I knew the time he would spend with me could be split into segments.

The first segment is always the price of milk, and he always gives me a hard time. The price of milk has come down 15 per cent since the beginning of the year, so why wouldn't he give me a hard time?

He can be quite aggressive and I think he might have a speech impediment because most of the words he used began with the letter F.

He first told me he needed more money for his milk, which I agreed with. I told him the price is related, like it or not, to what goes on in the wider world, the price of milk powder in New Zealand, the price of cheese in Ireland, things like that. He didn't agree with this but I know and he knows that this, unfortunately, is the case.

So we paused there, once he'd got that off his chest, and he asked for another cup of tea. I had one as well, which took my tea level up to somewhere around my eyes, (we serve a lot of tea, coffee and milk while communicating).

We were also serving toasted cheese sandwiches made with our own Pembrokeshire cheese (available in a supermarket near you) and he visibly relaxed as he ate his sandwich. Eventually he wiped a bit of melted cheese off his chin and leant forward to share a confidence and I knew we were moving on to segment two.

'There's a man in our village who is a contractor,' he said. He went on to tell me that this man only has one tractor, (contractors these days usually have more tractors than they can count, so having one is to put his story into context).

Every month the man has a financial crisis when the HP payment is due on the tractor.

'He comes to me to help him out now and again so at the moment he owes me three months' work that I've not yet identified,' said our co-operative member.

I asked how the hell did he manage with a crisis like that every month.

'You just have to keep your head down and your arse up and work away and hope for the best.'

He paused again, so that I knew we were moving on to segment three. Segments two and three were not unrelated, as I found out.

'There's some people from London bought a bungalow with three acres of land in our village, they were going to live off this land – good-lifers.'

The tone was scornful; he'd seen it all before – three goats and a patch of cabbages are not a living for anyone.

'Anyway, they have a septic tank for the bungalow which is about 200 yards down the field and the pipe between dwelling and tank gets blocked.

'They spend a couple of days with draining rods to no avail, so the contractor said he would clear the pipe for them. When they asked him how much it would cost he told them £500 and they accepted the offer, lavatorial arrangements having become quite difficult by now.'

For the contractor, these were riches beyond belief and would settle a couple of HP payments. So he hired a mini digger and assumed he would find the blockage, dig out a bit of pipe, replace it and be away. A day later he'd still not found the blockage and he could see his £500 ending up in the hands of the owner of the mini digger.

So he went to a farmer in the village and asked him to fill his slurry tanker with a load of water out of the river and bring it up to see if they could 'ease' the blockage. Slurry tankers usually fill themselves with vacuum, but what can suck can also blow.

So they took 1,500 gallons of river water up to the bungalow and fitted the discharge pipe to the blocked pipe down the field by the septic tank. The plan was for the contractor to go into the bathroom and for the farmer to send some water up the pipe. As soon as there was some clearance, the contractor was to phone the farmer on his mobile phone to tell him to stop.

So that's what they did.

Just to give you a better feel for this story but without going into too much detail, the water would have been pushing against what was in the blocked pipe already.

The first visible movement of liquid in the bathroom came up through the toilet with such force that it hit the ceiling and removed the polystyrene tiles. The contractor frantically tried to phone the farmer to stop him pumping but he couldn't get a signal on his mobile.

Not without some resource he put the toilet seat down and stood on it, only to be thrown across the bathroom.

He beat a retreat and ran outside to stop the farmer but it was too late – the contents of the pipe and 1,500 gallons of dirty river water went right through the bungalow and were coming out of the kitchen door.

To be fair to them both, they had cleared the blockage pipe.

That seemed like the end of that particular story, but it wasn't. The farmer's wife, who had probably heard the story countless times before, said: 'But you haven't told him who the farmer on the tanker was...'

And our member grinned sheepishly and beat a retreat out into the mud and the rain of the Royal Welsh show. The people in the bungalow went back to London a month later.

★ ★ ★

THERE'S a part of my life that takes me away from the farm for a few days most weeks. At this time of year I spend quite a lot of time at agricultural shows. I'm usually very busy but I do have the opportunity to indulge in one of my favourite occupations: watching the world go by. Human beings as a species come in all shapes and sizes and most of us are amazed at the variety we see. And I am always amazed at what people will buy at a show and then carry around with them for the rest of the day. Countless times I've seen husband and wife, often the large wife and small henpecked husband of the stereotypes we see in seaside postcards, wife leading the way, husband dutifully following, carrying something large and cumbersome like a loft ladder or an ironing board.

Yesterday, at the Royal Welsh, a man came past at 9.30am proudly carrying a new chainsaw. He walked past five times during the day, each time looking more weary. I was left with the thought that in more than 30° heat, if I was going to buy a chainsaw, I would buy it at about 5 o'clock, just before I went home.

At the show I heard the story of a lady farmer who had the misfortune to have a large travellers' camp next to her farm. She'd seen youths about with a crossbow and was fairly sure that they'd had two of her lambs, but was fairly pragmatic about it because she couldn't prove it and the police didn't seem very interested anyway, but she had smelt barbecued lamb on the wind one evening. When she found a foal with a crossbow bolt lodged in its leg, that was a different matter.

At first light next morning she was in the camp with an ornate bowl filled with water, sprinkling water around each caravan in turn and making weird chants. The occupants came tumbling out of their caravans to see what was going on but she continued her progress undeterred. The travellers phoned the police who carted our heroine away for disturbing the peace. (The irony of this will not be lost on any of us.) After a three-hour 'cooling off' period she was released and returned home to find the camp deserted. The occupants had fled because they thought she'd put a spell on them. What a brave lady, and clever with it.

* * *

IT'S A BIG day on the farm today. Today's the day I take Bill, our bearded collie to be clipped. A bearded collie in full coat looks a bit like a Herdwick sheep and ours is just about as much use as a Herdwick sheep at fetching the cows.

The best working dog I ever had was a bearded collie bitch. She was so clever and so good at what she did, she was a once-in-a-lifetime dog. I always used to clip her myself. She wouldn't allow me to use electric clippers, but she would lie flat out on her side for about 10 minutes once a day for me to snip away with Ann's best dressmaking scissors. After 10 minutes she'd had enough, would open her eyes and be away. You wouldn't be able to catch her again until the next day and as the actual clipping took many, many sessions, it was a very strange dog that would be about the yard for a couple of weeks.

I always used to leave her head and neck until last, which made her look like a lion. I think she quite liked that. One of the problems for a long-haired dog that spends its day around cows and cow muck is that quite a bit of the latter sticks to your coat, so that, come the dry weather, all these little bits of coat have what I call clinkers on them that rattle as you go about your daily routine.

To digress, I've always had a bit of a weakness for different animals, that's why, in a herd of about 190 dairy cows there are some Ayrshires, some Jerseys, some Dairy Shorthorns and some Brown Swiss. There are about 175 conventional black and white cows but I do like to see a few different sorts as well.

When I kept sheep, I occasionally had some Herdwick. They are a native breed of the Lake District and, when I say I had them occasionally, it was because I owned them but I couldn't keep them in. One day I was driving to a speaking engagement in the Lake District and, three miles from home, I passed three Herdwick ewes marching down the road in single file. 'There's a coincidence,' I thought, 'Me driving to the Lake District and seeing Herdwick sheep on the road.' I ignored the fact that they were mine and kept on driving. They were back at home when I returned next day.

Anyway, I arrive at the vet's where the dog trimmer sets up shop twice a week. The lady groomer rolls her eyes when she sees Bill (funny how women do that) but she likes him really, and apparently he stands on the table as good as gold for the two or three hours this all takes. I think he actually enjoys the fuss, and the freedom from a hot coat. The coat is so dense that the piece that comes off his back hangs together like a fleece. I ask the lady to leave a tuft of hair at the end of his tail, Bill would like to look like a lion as well, but we get a bit more eye-rolling, and when I fetch him there's no tuft.

The dog I take home has been transformed. Everyone who comes on the yard for the next week thinks we've got a new dog, he bears absolutely no resemblance to the dog of the day before. I think he misses his warm coat at nights; no more sleeping on the doorstep, he's under a bush in Ann's shrubbery, but no need for you to tell her that.

It's not all positives for Bill. The other dogs don't recognise him so they want to fight him to establish where everyone sits in the pecking order. This doesn't take long as he was always at the bottom anyway. Next morning he comes with me to fetch the cows, which is unusual. They don't recognise him either so they all want to chase him.

While my border collie Mert is away around the boundaries of the field getting the furthest away cows into motion Bill decides he will help as well. It's quite strange how he behaves; he fixes a stare on the nearest cow, goes down on his belly, and stalks her. To use the lion analogy again, that's exactly how he does it. He stalks the cow until she, or he for that matter, bottles out. It's usually the cow, then he chases her for a few yards before he moves on to stalk the next one. If I were to rely on this process to collect 190 cows it would take all day, so I'm not sorry when he loses interest after a couple of days and Mert and I don't have to witness this morning pantomime. Bill? He stays on the yard and goes back to being fat and lazy which he does really well.

While I've been writing this, I've had one eye on the pond in the field in front of our house. A few days ago, a mallard came out with six ducklings and I find myself counting them all the time. When mother duck takes her brood out on to the field they are always accompanied by a pair of carrion crows or a pair of ravens. These birds busy themselves at a safe distance, affecting nonchalance as you've never seen it affected before. But I know what they are really there for and so does mother duck.

When the brood are on the pond they are much more mobile and I can see them now darting about like so many little jet-ski riders. But they're not safe here either. Also busy in the background are a pair of coots who will go under water and take a duckling from below the surface. This is how most of the ducklings will disappear because mother can't see the attack coming. It's all dramatic stuff, a bit like an avian version of Jaws.

★ ★ ★

THE BIG JOB lately is getting our maize crop planted. There's just a bit more to it than that. Maize is a crop that thrives on plenty of manure.

Ours gets plenty of that but that, in itself, is a big job. Carting muck to the chosen field and then spreading it all is very time-consuming, but well worth it.

Over the years I have come to learn that carrot is usually better than stick, so I try to generate some enthusiasm to get the job done. Suggestions that 'Bank holidays are so busy you're all better off working,' get a mixed reception. 'If you work late tonight I'll go and fetch us some chips,' is better received. No-one who works here is ever asked to do anything that David and I wouldn't do, so yesterday I spent all day with our youngest worker spreading chicken muck.

Things had gone well all day, so that at 7 o'clock I said I'd pop for 10 minutes into our local town to fetch fish and chips and something to drink. Standing in the queue in the chip shop, thinking about the tons of chicken muck we'd spread that day, and what good it would transmit to the subsequent maize crop, I realised it had gone quiet and everyone was staring at me, except for the proprietor.

He was scowling – but it was probably him that has got to clear up the mucky footprints in his shop. He was probably hoping the smell would disappear when I did.

* * *

DOGS ARE clever, my dog Mert is very clever. I use the word 'my' deliberately because, as a farm dog, he used to be everybody's dog, but over the last few weeks he's become my dog. Most weeks I have to go away, sometimes for a couple of days at a time. During these absences he has taken to lying by the kitchen door until I come back and refusing to move.

He's developed that even further just lately by refusing to go with anyone else to fetch the cows, even if I'm at home. This has made him quite unpopular but no-one is going to do anything about it because he will soon curl his lip up and show his teeth just to emphasise his position.

When I'm at home he's always with me and it's amazing how he develops as a working dog. Our cows are milked in two batches and, without going into detail, the yard has to be cleared of one batch before you let the second batch go. To clear the yard properly, you have to look up each row of stalls to make sure you haven't missed a cow lying down somewhere. He's watched me do this countless times and now he does it on his own.

If there's anyone about, I can now have this sort of conversation with him because he will quite automatically go up each row of the sheds in turn. I lean on a gate and say 'just go and check that next row', which he was going to do anyway but it makes it look as if he's understood what I said. The 'audience' usually consists of people who he won't even fetch the cows with, so they get a bit tetchy about all this.

We have to be extra vigilant on clearing the yard because, a few weeks ago, I bought a fresh calved Jersey heifer at a sale. She turned out to be a lot smaller than I thought and, as she's a bit of a free spirit, she will often go off on her own to lie down in the sheds somewhere.

When Mert is busy on his shed-clearing, you actually think all the cows have gone and he's just double-checking, when this Jersey heifer will come trotting out. She looks more like a fallow deer than a cow. When I bought her I christened her Peggy because she looks a bit like a girl I was at school with, but Bambi would have been more appropriate.

* * *

WITH ALL the cats busy rearing kittens, it has surprised me how many rats we have about here. My assessment comes from the numerous rat remains that I find about. The cats are obviously giving the rats a hard time, which is excellent. Funny things rats: people react to them in different ways, from total fear to total hatred. My son is dead scared of them. I once went round a corner to where my son and an employee were tidying up a shed to find them both standing on five gallon cans while a family of rats that they had disturbed scurried about looking for a new home.

They've never bothered me. I was tidying up the mangers for the cows the other day and came upon the back-end of a rat busy sorting out the silage for bits of corn. He soon found himself underneath my welly – some people would have run the other way.

* * *

I HAVE alluded in the past to the issue of producer milk prices. This topic has gained prominence recently because of the interest shown by the Women's Institute, and good luck to them and thank-you. Some of the headline-grabbing statements from major retailers have led people to the view that we've all had a 4p increase in our returns, and the job is done.

Just to put things into some sort of perspective, I have just had a price increase of a quarter of a penny per litre and I am still getting less for my milk than I was 12 months ago. What should worry consumers is the fact that milk powder (dried milk) is trading on world markets at higher prices than are available to us from selling our milk into a liquid dairy or a cheese factory. We have been told for years that we have to accept what the market will return.

Well, the market now gives us an alternative option and the boot is finally on the other foot. If the UK wants UK milk, it will have to pay the market price for it.

* * *

MORE TIME spent on a tractor of late means more time to observe what is going on around you, and this time of observation has led me to the conclusion that it isn't necessarily that wonderful being a pheasant.

Cocks and hens lead very different lives at this time of year. The hen pheasants have secreted themselves away in hedgerows sitting on eggs. Measuring their success at this, in terms of the numbers of young pheasants that they will actually rear, would suggest that this is a complete waste of time and contributes very little, apart from so many ready meals for carrion crows and the like.

Once or twice a day your hen pheasant will make her way off her nest to look for some sustenance and is promptly sexually assaulted by every cock pheasant within about 50 yards. How they actually survive this period amazes me, but survive they mostly do.

The cock pheasants, for their part, are showing signs of wear and tear. They patrol what they think of as their own territory, but are under constant attack from their neighbours. Most of them are now limping as a result of all the fighting and their beautiful spring plumage is starting to lose its sheen. They spend three months of the winter being shot at and the next four months fighting. It's true that they spend quite a lot of that four months trying to make love, but it never seems to lead to any meaningful relationships. I think if I were a cock pheasant I would be smoking about 40 a day by now.

On the shoot next door, the keeper has taken to rearing a particularly dark strain of pheasant, darker even than the ones I call melanistic. A small colony of these has made its way on to our shoot, probably about two miles. The birds keep themselves very much to themselves and seem to live their lives to a higher moral standard than I see elsewhere in the pheasant world.

* * *

THE 'NEW' world of environmental benefits in farming is starting to make an impact. Several hundred yards of new hedgerow has been planted on this estate during the winter and it is pleasing to see how much of it has established itself successfully.

Farmers and landowners are paid to put in these new hedges, just as a generation or so ago they were paid to remove them, further evidence, if it were needed, of what a mad world we live in. As for me, I see all this going on and shrug my shoulders at it. I've never taken a hedge out in more than 40 years of farming. I'm quite proud of that, seems I was right all along.

* * *

TURKEYS, it was always said, are compulsively suicidal. If, for example, a young turkey in a rearing shed should die, another turkey would come and lie down next to it. Then another would do the same, and another and another, so that in no time at all there would be a whole heap of turkeys.

Unfortunately, the ones at the bottom of the pile would be suffocated by those on the top, so it would be possible to progress from one dead turkey to lots and lots of dead turkeys in no time at all.

There is something of the death-wish about all livestock. We had a cow that had a difficult calving recently that left her a bit wobbly on her back legs. We put her out in what we call the stack yard where she could lie under cover should she wish and where there were several patches of fresh grass to nibble. Most importantly she was off the concrete and on natural ground where she could find her feet at all times and recover. I was working up there all afternoon and twice she made her way 30 yards or so to the water trough, ate some of the silage we had put out for her and then, each time, returned to a cosy spot in the corner under the hedge to lie down. Because of the work we were doing, there were no gates to keep her in but given her condition and her obvious contentment with where she was, I was not particularly concerned.

During the night she became more adventurous and she wandered further afield. She declined the opportunity to go into our garden, by two different gateways, as she did the gardens of our two immediate neighbours. She rejected the chance to go into my son's garden through the small wicket gate, but decided instead to try to enter his garden over his cattle grid where she spent most of the night with her legs firmly stuck between the bars.

Fortunately, we have the kit on farms these days to lift cows out of situations like this without too much trouble. Her back legs, which were a problem after the calving, are fine now, but one of her front legs is now badly swollen.

We've only ever had a cow stuck in a grid once before. That was on a Sunday afternoon and the incident occurred on some land we were renting about a mile away. A passer-by came on the cow in the grid and telephoned 999. You might have spotted by now that we live in a very rural area populated by very rural people, most of whom have a very good idea of what goes on and how things all 'work'.

The local volunteer firemen 'scrambled' to the call. They knew immediately where the field was, and whose cattle were in the field. They also knew which pub my son was in so they drove there first of all, blue lights and sirens busy, collected my son, took him in the fire engine to help them extricate the cow, which they soon did, and then, at a more leisurely pace, returned him to the pub and his pint.

★ ★ ★

YOU MUST have 40 to 50 hares up on your top ground,' the keeper told me during one of our Saturday morning chats. He calls them 'my hares' because he knows I love to see them about.

I knew there were a lot of hares about, but had no idea there were that many. He has a much better idea than me, because he's been lamping for foxes lately and the hares sit still there in the spotlight for him to count.

If there are that many, and he's rarely wrong, I take great pride in it.

I've often been told that hares are a good barometer of the wellbeing of the countryside, so using that criteria, all's looking quite well. And they're not just any old hares; they all look fat and well.

I often come across four or five playing together, oblivious to the approaching Land Rover, so full of themselves that they will often look you right in the eye before they slope off. A neighbouring tenant has a different view on hares and phones the landlord's agent on a regular basis complaining about hare numbers. It takes all sorts!

Quite what damage they do to mature arable crops I don't

know, they are more likely to be grazing the short grasses on the field margins. But 'my' hares could be getting too numerous for their own good.

I drove around the stock and the fields on Saturday morning. It is one of my favourite jobs and it suited my plans the next day, the Sunday morning, to go around before breakfast. It had rained hard in the night and as soon as I went off the hard road onto the track and the field margins I could see the tracks of a four-wheel drive vehicle that had travelled there since I had the previous evening. I was able to follow its marks all around my land and it was quite a tour. I'm good at reading the signs, I even found where they'd got stuck and had to have another go. (I'm probably an Apache Indian reincarnated as an impoverished dairy farmer.)

I was concerned about who had been about. The keeper usually travels about on his quad bike and has a four-wheel drive vehicle as well, but a quick call on the mobile soon determined that it wasn't him.

The hares didn't behave as if someone has been 'having a go', you can soon tell, but someone could have been checking to see how many were about. A few years ago a gang used to go up on the top, hare coursing, perhaps they'd been back to have another look. At the moment the keeper shoots about three or four a year strictly for the landlord who will talk eloquently about the delights of jugged hare.

★ ★ ★

I'M NEVER quite sure of the right word; the word I'm looking for is litigious. I'm trying to find a word that best described the society we find ourselves in. It describes what some people call ambulance chasers, the people who appear on adverts on our television with: 'Have you had an accident at work?'

Of course I have, who hasn't, it's a part of life. When my son broke his ankle ice-skating last winter there were two 'suits' there getting him to sign disclaimers before the ambulance arrived, and who can blame them? This blame culture has manifested itself in a new way, one that will affect the countryside.

Apparently there are vigilant council employees out there, scrutinising roadside trees. The story goes like this; your council employee spots a tree with a couple of dead branches, it could be a large dead branch which could be dangerous and in need of removal, or it could be a tiny bit of dead branch, about a foot or so long.

A letter is sent to the owner of the tree, questioning the safety of the whole tree and giving the owner 28 days to do something about it, putting the responsibility for any future accidents firmly onto the owner.

The owner of the tree usually takes advice from a tree expert along the lines of 'Is this tree safe for ever?' Well no-one in his right mind is going to say 'yes' to that. Around here there are 26 healthy oak trees marked up for felling with red crosses on them. There is an established paper trail of passing the buck that ultimately ends with the tree being cut down. If a farmer were to fell 20 trees somewhere it would probably lead to an outcry. But for Health and Safety, it's apparently OK. No-one wants to see anyone injured by a falling tree, or bough, especially me, but this is all a bit over the top. Where's the commonsense, where's the balance?

The past weeks have seen us out and about on our land on a daily basis, as the seasons and the work progresses. After all these years, I still find the views from our top fields remarkable and remind myself on a daily basis how lucky I am to live and work in such an environment. I took some sandwiches and a drink up to our young tractor driver the other day and took the opportunity to take it all in, while I waited for the tractor to go around the field and come back to the gateway. When he got off the tractor I told him that we'd got it all wrong, I suggested that it was ridiculous that I was paying him to drive up and down this particular field on such a lovely sunny day, with panoramic views that some people would envy. I went on, quite eloquently, to suggest that it would be much fairer if he paid me for the privilege of doing what he was in such surroundings. He took a sip of tea, thought about it a bit, and said he would rather leave things as they were.

* * *

LAST SUNDAY was the Bank Holiday weekend. You probably want to forget it. It didn't stop raining here all day, it wasn't a day to do much, I did a couple of hours of essential work after breakfast, came back and watched *Country File*, slept in the chair for an hour, fought off thousands of Zulus on the television and set off around the stock while afternoon milking was in progress. It was still raining heavily and some way off the council road, on a farm track I came upon a minibus backed well under a tree and almost out of sight.

Mindful that someone might be after 'my' hares, I thought to myself: 'Aha, I bet these are up to something.' And I was right, they were up to something, but nothing that hares or rabbits needed to worry about.

* * *

HOT WEATHER and goats. It's all changed now, yesterday morning I was actually looking for a pullover because it was, in relative terms, chilly. But throughout July it was as hot as we've known it, and on some hot sticky nights it was difficult to sleep. There is an age-old solution to this that goes all the way back to Adam and Eve if you follow my drift, sleeping on top of the bed without night attire.

A friend of mine was regaling us with this solution one night in the pub. He's one of those farmers who has rarely been sighted without a cap on his head. Well, he's been seen at weddings and funerals without a cap on his head but it's always stuffed in his pocket. His ruddy weather-beaten countenance stops halfway up his forehead and becomes very white where his hair starts to recede. There was some discussion in the bar about the possibility that his 'naked' solution on hot nights did in fact include his cap, but he assured us it didn't, although the cap was on the table at the side of his bed.

And then there are your goats. I've never kept goats but many years ago, no, even longer than that, a lot of dairy farmers kept the odd goat running with their cows because goats carried a disease that was related to a similar disease that caused abortion in cattle. The presence of the goat helped the cattle to build up a natural immunity. The goats carried brucella melatensis — I've had a brain cell carrying that information locked up since I was in college — which was related to brucellosis in cattle, which we have now eradicated from our herds.

From casual observation I have come to the opinion that all goats are rascals. I think there is a part of them that yearns for the rocks and boulders of their ancestors. When Julie Andrews climbed every mountain, goats were right up there with her in spirit, leaping from rock to rock with abandon.

And so, for those of you still with me, I draw the stories of the goats and the hot weather together.

Our friend with the cap has made lots of mistakes in his life, as have we all, but well to the fore in these mistakes is allowing his daughter to keep two goats.

These two goats were chained up at night, but most nights managed to escape, dragging the chains behind them. Having achieved the escape bit the next essential for your frisky goat is to do a bit of leaping about on boulders. Most farms around here don't have boulders on the yard, but goats are inventive and imaginative creatures and if they can't find a boulder, what better than a five-year old Vauxhall Vectra?

So we return to our hero whose sleep is disturbed, on a bright sunny morning, by the sound of long lengths of chain being dragged across his car. The goats have decided it is great fun to jump on the boot of his car, then onto the roof and then off the bonnet down onto the ground. They take it in turns and then reverse the procedure.

My friend leaps out of bed, pausing only to put his cap on, and rushes to the bedroom window. He takes in the scene out on his yard in an instant and rushes downstairs, his bad language, legendary locally, now in full flow. He puts his wellies on at the back door and launches himself out onto the yard wearing just his cap and his wellies with nothing in between.

The goats aren't dull and are off around the corner at some speed with our hero in hot pursuit hurling abuse and anything else that comes to hand. There's a public footpath running through his yard and coming towards him are about 20 ramblers.

There are several aspects to this story among which are: goats that had the last laugh, ramblers that had a surprise and a farmer who inadvertently became a flasher, without the long mac.

* * *

I'M ON my daily round of the off-lying cattle. The 30 in this group are all lying down chewing their cud. I pull up next to the bull and switch the engine off. He's lying there contentedly in a soft bed of fresh grass and buttercups. He gives absolutely no acknowledgement of my presence, although I'm only a yard away. He continues cudding rhythmically, pausing only to swallow that particular mouthful and to replace it with another.

I sit and stare at him, and he steadfastly stares back. We've been together a long time, the bull and I, but there's never been a relationship developed. He knows what his job is and he leaves me to do mine. His is to eat, sleep and breed – an idyllic life. It seems a long time since that was my job as well.

He's a Limousin bull, his calves are easily born and we've used him on our heifers for their first calves for years. Every now and again, I introduce new maiden heifers to his harem as soon as they are old enough.

I'm not sure how old he is, I'd have to look at his passport, and I've not seen him 'perform' for years, but he certainly does, because in due course all the heifers start to develop their little bosoms and eventually go on to calve.

Although the calves are nice and small and easy to deliver, they go on to make excellent beef cattle, because we often sell a calf to a local farmer who has lost a calf off a suckler cow, and they are always very pleased with the sort of cattle they grow into.

They have also been heard to say that they can run so fast they don't know whether to fatten them for the butcher or send them to a trainer and enter them for National Hunt races. There's nothing in the bull's demeanour to suggest he could father race winners. I

reckon he must be 15 or 16 years old now, which is quite old for a working bull. If I ran him with more than 100 cows, he probably wouldn't last long, but where he is and what we expect of him seems to be well within his capabilities.

When I first bought him, we had a young lad working for us who asked what breed he was. 'Limousin'. 'Where do they come from?' 'They come from a region in France.' 'France eh, we'll have to call him Herman.'

I've never quite worked that one out, but Herman he's been ever since.

All cattle have passports now; it's an inevitable process to improve traceability after problems like foot and mouth, and BSE.

I know lots of farmers who've never been on holiday, never been on an aeroplane, never been abroad and never needed a passport. Their cattle all got one before they did.

★ ★ ★

I'VE BEEN on a tractor most of the last week, ploughing and working a field for a fresh seeding of grass. The family all reckon I like ploughing because I usually manage to work that job for myself. I usually find it relaxing, but this time it wasn't.

We'd spread a lot of muck on the field, and it was difficult to strike a balance between ploughing at a proper depth to bury the muck without the wheels spinning too much.

Working the field down is done in one pass, with a machine we call a power harrow, but that is a slow job in terms of miles per hour and it all gives you plenty of time for reflection and thought. It can be quite a lonely job on a tractor all day on your own. The radio is tuned to Radio 1, and I don't know how to change stations, so it stays firmly switched off.

This particular field is the first one I ever worked in that was my own field. I've ploughed it and worked it so many times since that I even recognise some of the worms. On that occasion, I was rolling the furrows down after someone else had ploughed it. And I was driving my first tractor, a Fordson Dexta, which was about three years old and cost me £600.

I remember that there was a flurry of snow that day that wet the ground so much that it clogged the roller, and I had to pack in. I'm pretty sure I can remember how cold I was because we didn't have the cabs and the clothing we have now.

For company today, as I plough, I have four cock pheasants, four jackdaws and a seagull. I wonder what the seagull's name is. It's not easy, as I don't know what sex it is. It's bound to have a name, all the animals in the nature programmes have names – lions, cheetahs, even meerkats. It looks like a Dougal.

For a land-based gull, my tractor and plough turning up worms is probably his equivalent of a trawler returning to harbour and throwing bits of fish overboard.

It's a very hot day, and none of our tractors are of an age that means they have air conditioning. I have to choose between having the windows shut and slowly roasting or have the windows open and sitting in fresher air that is dust-laden. Still, a bit of hardship never hurt anyone and when I walk across the yard later on covered in dust everyone thinks I've been working really hard.

I have my tea, shower and read the farming papers in the garden. It's almost like being in heaven – except we haven't got any decent garden furniture to sit on, and I'm wearing shorts and the dogs keep licking my legs.

* * *

THERE'S QUITE a decent shed in one particular field so most years we put some turnips in it and use it and the shed to overwinter about 10 heifers. In the spring we scatter a few grass seeds on the field to provide some grazing for calves, but come July we plough it again and put in some more turnips.

It looks a bit untidy at this time of year because what is left of last winter's turnips has run away to seed. The landlord drives past there every day so it wouldn't hurt to tidy it up a bit, so I put on the machine we use to trim the fields and venture forth.

It turns out that this field is a bit of a wildlife sanctuary. There's quite a few pairs of partridge in there, the inevitable pheasants and a lot of tiny rabbits – what they are doing out and about at that age goodness only knows, they should be at home with mum. But what really surprised me was the number of half-grown leverets.

As you progress over a field, as I was, the wildlife usually keeps moving on into the bits you haven't cut yet, so you have to be careful you don't count the same leveret twice, but there were lots of different sizes of leveret. I'm sure it wasn't the same one going round and round the field doing a lap of honour.

I reckon there were 10 or 12 there in a nine-acre field, a sort of hare crèche if you like. My activities have put an end to that but I'm not too worried, there's an abundance of cover about at this time of year in the adjoining cornfields and in the heavy crops of second-cut silage.

On the other hand, being fond of wildlife can come back and bite you – and it has. We have two fields of maize this year, and about 10 days ago I walked them both to see what sprays they needed. Maize is an expensive crop to grow; the seed alone can cost more than £40 an acre. Apart from providing a very high energy feed for the cows, which complements grass silage in the mixed diet we give them, it has the particular advantage of growing well in a dry summer. A dry summer is our Achilles heel, because ultimately it's all about having enough tons of fodder for nearly 300 mouths to eat for six months of the year.

So maize is a very important crop for us. It thrives on plenty of farmyard manure so we spend days and weeks carting plenty of that. It's the tallest, most robust plant that most of us grow, yet ironically, it will not cope with any competition. It's critical to get the spray right because it won't compete with weeds.

When I walked the fields to decide what sprays to use, it was coming up well with a good plant population. As I passed the one field where I always keep an eye on wildlife, as far as I could make out there were four pheasants regularly there, two hares and 19 rooks. I watch the rooks in particular because they can play hell with a maize field.

They will dig out the seed when you sow it and they will pull out the young plants as they grow. But 19? Not a big problem. There's usually 19 birds of some sort in any field at any time. When I walked the field again this week to see if it was ready to spray, to say I was dismayed would be the understatement of the year. Huge areas of maize had been decimated, mostly plants about six inches high pulled out.

The crop is in effect, a write-off. I don't know what this has cost me in terms of time and effort but it will certainly be in the thousands of pounds.

Over the years you get used to setbacks like this but in today's dairy industry, with finances in such a parlous state, this is a huge body blow. Part of the therapy in coping with this particular reversal is to think: 'What are you going to do about it?'

My first reaction was to start all over again with a fresh crop of maize but it's getting very late for that and would be a gamble I can't now afford to lose. We've decided to work the ground up again and sow a variety of very fast-growing ryegrass. It should grow us a crop in about six weeks and with luck another after that. Our priority now has to be accumulating enough tons of silage for the winter.

We will have less feed value but it's no good having high feed-value silage if it is all finished by the end of January. My friend, the keeper, has just been on the phone. He shot four or five of the rooks yesterday and opened their crops up. They were full of leatherjackets (cranefly, daddy-long-legs) and slugs. So there we have it, the rooks are digging for slugs and grubs, the slugs and grubs are feeding on the maize plants and up they come. In their way, the rooks were trying to help.

* * *

THERE IS a part of my life that takes me to London most months. I always travel by the train from Birmingham to Euston. Farmers are strange travellers – they look in every field as they go by and assess the crops and livestock.

I've done this journey so many times that I recognise every field as I pass it and know what crops are where and how they are progressing. I often wonder what normal people look at as they travel. What struck me was that I saw only one dairy herd in the fields during the whole journey.

It was milking time on the way back but I don't think I missed any others. I saw one field with a nice bunch of black and white heifers but couldn't see their mums anywhere.

There were a few beef cattle and sheep about but not in any big numbers. What is for sure is the fact that there were a lot more horses than cattle. What we will eat if there's a famine, goodness only knows – horses? Going to London is something I've done only over the last few years and I never knew it very well.

I always use taxis when I get there, it helps me to get to know London and the taxi drivers know their way around better than me.

I don't reckon much to tube trains. I wouldn't put animals on them and you never know who's down there. A simple country boy like me could end up in the white slave trade or as a rent boy.

* * *

I GOT BACK from band parade last Sunday reconciled to the fact that my Sunday sleep in the chair was going to be curtailed by at least 50 per cent. One of the worst parts of being a dairy farmer is that I'm always tired.

An hour or two in my armchair on Sundays is quite precious. I've had a bad sort of a week. But then I haven't had much of a life, either. I'm no stranger to heartbreak. It all started with the school fete.

We've always supported the local primary school, especially when our children were there. I was successively chairman of the PTA, a governor and chairman of governors.

Now our granddaughter is at the school, so when we were asked if we would host the summer fete, there wasn't much hesitation.

Of course, I knew all along what it was all about – me doing some gardening and tidying up. But I was fairly philosophical about that as well. Sometimes you need something specific to push you into making the extra effort, and the benefits obviously last beyond the function itself. Some farmers regularly host farm walks for other farmers. The only time that our place was tidy enough for that was the day my daughter got married.

However, I don't know if any of you have noticed, but it hasn't actually been very good weather for gardening lately. I haven't cut the lawns for nearly a fortnight. With only two days to go, I had to make a start. And a good start it was too.

The lawnmower's battery was flat, so I had to put it on charge for an hour. An hour later, it started first time, went 10 yards and stopped and refused to start again. There was petrol coming through OK so it must have been the spark plug. We tried the three spark plug sockets that we had but none fitted. Our next-door neighbour had two different ones to ours but they didn't fit either.

The young lad who works here occasionally goes into town at

lunchtime so I asked him to call at the people I bought the mower from to buy one. But, when he came back after lunch, he reported that they didn't have one either.

We called on another neighbour who used to work with chainsaws in the woods and he eventually got the plug out with a spanner – it was a bit like doing keyhole surgery with a shovel. We cleaned the plug, and the mower started up first time.

The youngster I referred to earlier used to come here one day a week on day-release from school. We've never allowed him to drive anything, but he's left school now and it's about time he made a start. I set him off and left him to it as I went to fetch the cows.

While I was away, it started to rain heavily and, when I got back, it was too wet to cut the grass. But I could always strim the long grass around the edges instead. I put a coat and hat on and started it up.

After about two minutes it stopped and refused to start again. For a minute, I wondered just how far I could throw it.

The next day, I tried to mow the lawns again. The mower went a few yards and then stopped. In desperation, I phoned the dealer – things were starting to get a bit serious now. He discovered the petrol tank was half full of water.

The lawns were eventually cut and when the big day arrived, I watched the young mothers busy themselves setting up their stalls. One of the mothers I'd not seen before looked particularly attractive, so I sauntered across to give her the benefit of my rustic charm.

Before I could get beyond introductions she told me that she was not that happy about holding the fete on a dairy farm because she was a vegetarian and a vegan and, as such, she knew that dairy cows were shut in sheds all the year round behind bars and never got out to enjoy the sun in grassy fields.

Well, that was straight to the point – no hidden agenda there. I struggled a bit with this as, over her shoulder, about 30 yards away, 48 cows were lying in a grassy field sunning themselves, and down the fields another 96 cows were doing exactly the same thing.

I didn't bother to point this out because there are none so blind as those who don't want to see. She obviously had such a blinkered view of things agricultural that my efforts would have been wasted.

Meanwhile, in our little town we have a carnival every year. Every year there is a theme for floats and shop windows. This year it was nursery rhymes. Last night I was talking to the manageress of an estate agent's. She said she had chosen *The House That Jack Built*. She searched the internet and found a picture of a shack in the US.

It was the sort of thing you see in Westerns; timber-built, up on stone piers. But this one had a roof that was caving in and a tree growing out of the chimney. It even had a rail across the front to tie up the horses. She put her display in the shop window but had to remove the photograph after the first morning because two couples had come in separately and asked for details.

★ ★ ★

IF ANYONE asks me, in greeting, how I am, I have a bad habit of saying: 'I'm struggling.' I hadn't given it much thought until I read a book devoted to positive presentation.

To say you are struggling is very negative – it's much better to say: 'I'm really well thank you, things are good, how are you?' If you had said that as a dairy farmer, over recent years, to anyone who knew anything about dairy farming, that person would presumably have thought you very positive but a liar.

But this year on the farm has been a bit of a struggle. We started the year with my son off work for eight weeks with a broken ankle. We had the most benign April any of us can remember, then we had the monsoon season, which not only went on and on, but finished with a sort of crescendo of floods and damage.

Weather we can usually cope with, but then our only full-time employee has been absent from work for about 10 weeks now, having suffered a stroke. I'm away on business two or three days most weeks, so when my son David has about 90 per cent of his help missing, struggle is the right word.

Caring for and milking our animals comes first; where we are off the pace is with all the repairs, renewals and tidying up jobs that we can usually catch up on during the summer. Recent August days have had an autumnal feel to them, so how far away is winter and its heavy workload?

Most people who work here become good friends and part of the family, so Jim's recovery is uppermost in our minds. We certainly miss him coming around the corner every day.

* * *

ON PREVIOUS occasions I have mentioned milk prices. Well, they are finally turning the corner. We haven't exactly found the end of the rainbow but it now seems likely that the price of milk, as it leaves farms, will return to levels we haven't seen for 10 years. How many industries would herald the prices of 10 years ago as a triumph?

What it does signal is an end to food price deflation. This movement of milk price is driven by a world marketplace that is in turn driven by an increase in the consumption of dairy products, in Asia in particular, that is all part of a move to an improved diet by millions of people.

For too long, dairy businesses in this country have thrived on the ability to buy cheap milk; from now on, if they want a dairy business, they will have to be able to pay the price or they will not have their raw material.

We also produce chicken here and I read a recent article last week about a major supermarket selling fresh chicken by the hundreds of thousands for £2. That's all very well for the consumer, but it completely avoids reality and gives the wrong impression of the value of food.

We pay about 25p for day-old chicks and that's when you are buying 50,000 at a time. We make just under 4p a bird before gas, electric, water and labour. Where's the long-term sense in that?

★ ★ ★

I KEEP telling myself that I won't write about the weather but weather is such a big part of farming life that I can't avoid it. It's Sunday morning, 7 o'clock, and I've just watched the cows go off to their daytime grazing — off they go with a spring in their step and with a clear sense of purpose. This is a daily triumph for optimism over reality because when they get to their daytime fields there is no grass there. By 12 o'clock they will be on their way back because they know there will be a feed of silage and beet pulp waiting for them.

They are consuming silage in ever-increasing quantities while all around, grazing fields are assuming the dry, brown look that we call burning. When this happens in July, it usually means that the grass will not green over until September with its longer nights, heavier dews and, hopefully, some rain. They are forecasting even higher temperatures for the next few days, thank you very much, but one lesson I learned many years ago is that there's no point in agonising about things over which you have no control. So I'll just have to make the best of it, as usual.

I've mentioned at the onset of our calving season, calf-feeding is now a big job. Last winter, I bought a plastic calf-feeder. It's like two big bowls that are joined at their bases. One bowl acts as a base and the other bowl holds the milk and has 20 teats fitted to it. I suppose it looks a bit like an egg-timer. You tip the milk into the top half and the calves all suckle the teats. Sounds simple doesn't it? It isn't. You would think that the calves would all fan out around the feeder in a uniform way, but they don't. They all suckle at an angle as if they were side on to their mother's flank. This in itself shouldn't be a problem either, but an important part of the suckling process, if you are a calf, is to give the teat a bit of a bunt now and again.

The feeder is quite big; it stands about 3ft 6in tall and is about the same across. If there are 20 calves to feed, I put in about 10 gallons of milk. So we've got about a ton of calves, a lot of milk and, as if at some unseen given signal, all the calves give the feeder a combined push. The problem with this is that one half of the feeder screws into the other. Some days they all push clockwise; this is fine because it just tightens the two halves together, but some days they all push the other way around, which starts to unscrew things. My aim is to get the 10 gallons of milk into the calves. If everything comes apart, the 10 gallons of milk will soon be on the floor and I will have to start all over again.

In the next pen to the calves that star in the twice-daily pantomime of me trying to feed them, is a very different calf. This is a black and white heifer calf born about five weeks premature. It's smaller than my border collie but I've decided I will rear it. It's always been fundamental to my life as a farmer that I will do my best to keep things alive. It's a firmly held principle that is nothing to do with profit. In fact, time and time again, it has proved to be a very costly principle. Apart from being tiny, and to a degree emaciated, this little calf has shrunken, crinkled ears, so altogether it looks a poor thing. When I go to feed the calves, it struggles to its feet and so far gives itself a bit of a stretch. This is always a particularly good sign. I've got it on a diet of warm milk, glucose and an egg twice a day — my wife hasn't spotted the egg deficit yet. As soon as it has finished its food, it scuttles off to the corner of its pen and lies down until next feeding time.

This is quite a common phenomenon with calves. You often see it in calves that are born outside. They will have a feed and then hide themselves in some long grass or a clump of nettles. Sometimes you can spend ages looking for them. I think this particular calf is looking for somewhere to die but so far I haven't let it. If it survives it will acquire a name, probably related to the state of its ears, but the superstitious element in me says it is too soon, tempting providence, to give it a name.

* * *

I WAS on the tractor again yesterday in that field next to those neighbours who ignore me. It has become a bit of a challenge, try as I will, to catch their eye. I could blow the tractor horn but that would be too easy. One of them, the male, was trimming his boundary hedge so he was actually facing me; he kept his head lower and lower every time I passed. In the end, I was putting my head lower and lower as well, which was ridiculous. I bet I'd get his attention and his conversation if I drove into the hedge. I won't be beaten on this.

* * *

ON THE WILDLIFE front everything seems to have gone floppy with the heat. I took a friend for a ride around the fields and he was delighted to see so many hares about. On the basis that healthy hare populations are said to be a good indicator of a healthy countryside, I feel just a little bit proud. I have a saying that I usually trot out when things go wrong 'Just when you think things can't get any worse, they do.' Well, on the wildlife front, things have taken a turn for the worse.

A family of mink has been seen on the estate. Voracious killers, not just for food, but endless in their pursuit of birds and mammals. The damage they cause to wildlife is endless as well. Many are descendants of mink that were released into the wild by poor misguided souls who had no idea of the implications of what they were about. I can remember a time when there was a bounty on grey squirrels' tails. It's a pity that there isn't one today. Grey squirrels and mink were both introduced from elsewhere in the world and have no place here. I've never seen a red squirrel within 200 miles and I would love to see one as I went around the farm.

* * *

WE WERE one of the first to finish our silage around here and everyone is now catching up with the season and the delay caused by the wet weeks in May. Everywhere I look fields are being stripped of grass and sheep are being stripped of wool. We don't keep sheep anymore. I miss them but I don't miss the shearing. We never kept many sheep until I was about 50 years old, when we moved up to about 400 ewes. I thought it appropriate to learn to shear, which was quite late in life, but I did, and even sheared for other people occasionally.

We used to shear our ewes in the field and, unfortunately for me, the field was next to the pub. Two friends used to help me and, besides being paid to shear, my helpers used to think it appropriate that I took them to the pub for sausage and chips at lunchtime, plus a couple of pints. Large quantities of coke and lemonade were carried back in the afternoon and 'naturally' I would want to buy them a couple of pints when we finished in the evening. It used to be two hard days' work, plus wages, plus my tab at the pub.

One year, for various reasons, my help wasn't available and so I employed 'professional' shearers. We were finished by 3pm on day one. All I had done was sit on a bale and watched and then put a blue E on each ewe's backside as it was finished. It cost me about half of what it was costing before, I hadn't broken sweat and my back didn't feel as if it was about to break in two!

After that salutary experience I used to use some young shearers from the rugby club. It was a Saturday job, again we were finished by 3pm, their wives and girlfriends knew all this but struggled to understand why their partners were still not home by midnight. There's something satisfying about being in a pub on Saturday evening, filthy with sheep grease and smell when everyone else is dressed up. They used to look down their noses at us, and turn their noses up at us when they smelt us, but as we'd been in the pub two or three hours by then we didn't care. It reminded them that they were drinking in a rural area.

A friend of mine went to shear two sheep that were owned by some 'newcomers' who had bought the two sheep to keep the grass down in a small orchard. The sheep were called Mary and Ivy. Mary had a little lamb, but then she always did, didn't she? My friend sheared Ivy first. 'Ivy hasn't had a lamb yet, Mr Jones.' 'No, I can see that.' 'Do you think she will have one this time?' 'No I don't. In fact, I don't think she ever will.' 'Oh dear, why ever not?' 'Well you see this little swelling in the middle of 'her' belly; well that's where 'she' pees. If a sheep pees there it isn't a female sheep, it's a male.' Ivy quickly became Ivor and as far as I know he's still alive and well and keeping the grass down in the orchard.

$$\star \star \star$$

I WAS reminiscing about the passing of our village blacksmith recently and inevitably my mind doesn't just stop there, it goes on and remembers stories of long ago that were passed down.

They were quite remarkable in the fun involved, given that

all those years ago the life of a farm labourer and his family must have been so difficult and the farmer employer would have a huge hold over a man, as almost all of them lived in a cottage that was tied to the job.

Step over the line and job and home could be gone in two weeks' time. But despite that, they did have fun and here is one of the stories.

At the other end of the village to the blacksmith was a cottage that had with it three acres or so of ground. For the time, that ground was, compared with the lot of the farm worker, riches beyond belief.

If life was hard, and it was, there would be some envy and resentment – and the lucky man who had the bit of ground wasn't particularly nice anyway.

Every year this man would watch the progress of the hay harvest on the farms around the village. Most of these farms were of 400 or 500 acres and might employ five men.

As the hay harvest was drawing to a close he would get someone to mow his hay crop and over the following days he would turn it twice a day by hand. With immaculate timing it would be ready just as everyone else had finished, so it had become traditional for most of the men in the village to go to his field after tea with pitch forks, they called them pickles around here, and gather it up by hand and carry it forkful by forkful to the barn and put it safely into the dry.

It might sound an impossible job in today's mechanical world but there might be 10 or 12 of them and in three or four hours of very hard work they would have the job done.

They would all be paid on the night and it became tradition for them all to walk the mile or so to the nearest pub and no doubt they would drink all the money they had earned that evening. But why not? And good luck to them.

But one year things didn't turn out as expected. When they lined up to be paid, the pay was less than the year before. The resentment and envy festered to the surface and harsh words were exchanged. The man with the field wasn't to be moved – he had all sorts of excuses and it wasn't the usual jolly crowd that made its way to the pub that night.

Instead of the drink and the company lifting their mood, they became more morose and when they walked back down the lane at 10pm, revenge was in the air.

Unfortunately for the man with the field, it was a beautiful moonlit night. The labourers paused at his gateway to collect their pitchforks, looking at the cleared field and smelling the new hay sweet and safe in the barn.

Into the field they went and over the next three hours they carried all the hay back out of the barn and put it back in the rows in the field just exactly as it had been when they arrived that evening.

You can only imagine the reaction of the man with the field when he went to the gate next morning. He must have done what is sometimes described as a double take. His mind must have gone through a rapid sequence: who did this; why did they do it; what am I going to do now; and more importantly, what's the weather forecast?

He had to go from cottage to cottage seeking help. Everyone was expecting him but they made him grovel. And then there was the matter of payment to decide.

The hay was returned safely to the barn that night, none the worse for its adventures. The men had two nights in the pub that week, and a good story to tell, too.

* * *

ON ALTERNATE Fridays I have to take calves to market. I usually arrive at market by 11.15am for an 11.45am start but these starts have been delayed recently because it's the time of year when people sell ewes and where I go to market, the ewes are sold before the calves. It's no good being impatient, so I lean on a gate and watch the sheep trade.

The market for sheep has never been better: driven by our currency that has helped exports, against the New Zealand currency that hasn't helped their exports. If you spot a sheep farmer today it's just about as close as you will ever get to seeing a happy farmer.

In today's market place they take a trailer load of sheep to market and they can't get all the money in the same trailer to get it home.

Yesterday I watched them selling the Clun Forest rams. Forty to 50 years ago, the Clun was the most popular breed of sheep in the UK. Now it's something of a rarity on farms. Traditionally I think there were more than 30 breeds of sheep in the UK and on top of that, endless permutations of crosses. These days the most popular cross is called a North Country Mule, which is a cross between a Blue Faced Leicester ram and a Swaledale ewe, but there are Scots Mules, Welsh Mules and just about everything else you can think of.

When the champion Clun ram came into the ring yesterday I thought it would make about £300. It made £310. I thought to myself that I wasn't involved in sheep but I was spot on as a sheep valuer!

I was reading a history of the Cluns recently. On one day in 1928, I think it was, there were 22,000 sold on one day in Craven Arms. Two days later a different firm of auctioneers had a similar large sale in the same town.

In those days, all the sheep were walked in to the sale and the historians noted that there were so many flocks of sheep being driven down the valley from the Clun Forest area to Craven

Arms that shepherds arriving at junctions to the main road would sometimes have to hold their sheep back for 20 minutes before there was a gap in the procession sufficient for them to join.

Years ago I was in the area and had a day shearing Clun ewes within sight and sound of Clun church. There's not many of us left who can say that.

* * *

WE ARE not big on spraying on this farm, particularly on grassland, preferring not to do it at all. This is mainly because, in removing docks and thistles, you remove clover as well.

But eventually we have to go in with spray and in the following years we put some clover seed in with the fertiliser and hopefully put the clover back.

The only grass field we've had to spray this year is a seven-acre field on our boundary. Thankfully it's on everyone else's boundary as well, because it's well out of sight from all directions.

Because we want the spray to work properly we can't take the topper in there to trim it so when I had to go in there last week to fetch the cows I was ashamed of it. There were dead stalks of thistles everywhere and clumps of nettles in all their glory.

It's a theory of mine that nettles will one day take over the world – the spray we use for thistles checks nettle but it only gives them a headache and in a couple of weeks they are back on full power.

So it was with great delight that I gave it a really good tidy up. I gave it the agricultural equivalent of the No.3 you would get at the hairdressers.

I don't think there will be any thistles in there next year and I have plans for the nettles.

But it's amazing what you see when you are on a tractor. After spraying I drove slowly back to the gate and there, sitting on the top bar, also admiring what I'd done, was a hen turkey. I should add that I was nearly two miles away from where I see wild turkeys quite regularly and I've never seen one there before.

I turned the tractor off and sat and watched her and she, in turn, watched me. I watched for ten minutes and as far as I could see she was on her own. When I eventually drove on I wondered what a lonely life she must live, going about her business on her own with one eye looking for a fox.

I quite like the idea of turkeys being about and contemplated Christmas and taking my grandchildren out to find a Christmas tree and a turkey dinner on Christmas Eve. It's a Christmas card vision but it's not for here.

Our Christmas tree goes up in the middle of November and the state my wife gets in at Christmas, you'd have to shoot your turkey at least a week before if she was to feather it properly.

* * *

Autumn

THE ONSET of autumn brings a different look to the countryside. Having taken 90 acres of third-cut silage, and with all neighbouring corn crops now cleared, the land is in a way denuded, all the wrapping has been taken off and the wildlife is there for all to see.

As we've taken previous silage crops there has always been a crop of some sort adjacent to it that was convenient as a cover for disturbed wildlife. The only cover now are the blocks planted to provide food for wildlife in the winter.

My top land is splendidly isolated, but the autumn brings more visitors to it than at any other time of the year. Mainly they are contractors who arrive to do the silage. First up is the man who cuts all the grass. A former national ploughing champion, he does, as you would expect, a very tidy job.

I stop him for a chat; we talk about the crop and then he says: 'Boy, you've got some hares up here. I haven't seen so many hares for a long time.' It's inevitable that he should see them; the man with the mower does most of the 'disturbing' that goes on. When the gang arrives the next day to pick the grass up, I get similar comments from them.

The comments about the hares make me proud and pleased, almost like a parent at speech day. Not that I've done anything to help them to multiply but then, again, I've done nothing to hinder them either and, as you well know, I always keep a watchful eye over them.

My wife occasionally accompanies me around the fields in the evening and warns me of trouble to come if the hares eat her blackberries. It's not long before she will come up here on her own to pick them.

I sometimes think she is a humanoid squirrel and hoards them, because very few end up on any plate that I see. She must have a freezer full of them by now. Bare fields show me what the birds of prey are up to as well. Yesterday there was a buzzard as big as a turkey dining on a full-grown rabbit in the middle of a field.

On Sunday, there were two walkers on the footpath on the very top field. I always drive over to pass the time of day; this comes as a surprise to some, who see the approach of a farmer as a prelude to a ticking-off. They turn out to be Americans: 'Boy, you sure do have some big rabbits around here.' My hares are a bit of a focal point at the moment.

We're just about coming to the end of our harvesting. There's a scraggy field of maize to take home and we might have a bit of fourth-cut silage at the end of September, but we're on the last field of straw bales, and that seems to be coming to an end. I'm with my young assistant, I'm driving the loader, and he's supposed to be moving the trailer about the field from bale to bale.

It's normally him on the loader and me on the trailer, but we have a role-reversal because he says he's too tired to drive the loader today. This, as I load the bales, is a source of some reflection.

I must be 50 years older than him; I work much longer hours, yet he's tired. What really surprises me is the fact that he would admit to someone my age that he was too tired to do what he expects me to do. As I load the bales, there's not much movement of tractor and trailer to make my job any easier.

The field we are in is quite steep in places and it's not that easy to put a load on tidily. When we pull the full load on to a flat bit, it isn't tidy at all. It's 5.30pm by now, it's Friday evening, and my assistant is ready to go.

I won't let him go until we strap the load on further. I know from past experience that annoyance equals very fast tractor driving and we have to take this load through the village.

I'm not about to entertain the farming folk of the area by shedding a load of bales in the middle of the village, just as some of them are making their way to the pub, so we decide to leave the load in the field for the night. I drive the loader slowly home, but the other tractor is long gone in a cloud of black smoke.

★ ★ ★

SLOWLY, AND not very surely, because of the wet August, and thus far September, the combines are picking away at the harvest and oh-so-slowly, the fields become cleared.

This is an important time for the wildlife that was born this spring – in theory, birds and animals should be big enough by now to take care of themselves, although yesterday, when I got out of the truck to open a gate, I found the tiniest of leverets tucked away in the grass. It didn't move so I could see clearly that it would have nested comfortably in the palm of my hand.

We have several fields of third-cut silage to do at any time but, because we have refused to buy any more fertiliser at its present price, it's a fairly sparse crop. It provides cover of a sort but hares don't take much spotting in there and neither do the skylarks.

Skylarks concern me. Next to my passion for the brown hare, skylarks were the species I was most proud of, because there were lots and lots on our top land. But I would guess that there are less than half there now compared with three years ago, which is actually disgraceful because there must be 40 acres up there that are designated every year to wild birds. I don't know how much it costs because it's the landlord's stewardship scheme, but if it was working then birds should be increasing, especially skylarks, and not actually be in decline.

To my mind the reason is plain to see: buzzard numbers have trebled, in addition to the ravens and kites that we now see every day. All of these wreak havoc with songbirds, especially those that nest on the ground.

When did you last see a hedgehog? Badgers love hedgehogs – they roll them over and eat all the best bits in no time at all. Hedgehogs are predicted to be extinct in this country in 20 or 30 years but not to worry; someone will reintroduce them in 50 years' time.

The fact that we could intervene, but will never be allowed to, makes it all the more shameful. Not while we can always blame the farmers for everything.

* * *

AS I FOLLOW the daily routine of winter feeding, a routine that takes me mostly from one set of buildings to another (we just have a very few cattle out and they are on fields that we will need to plough in the spring, so it doesn't really matter if they do any damage to the sward), the fields are still littered with pheasants. But they are very different pheasants to those that were about a few months ago. Those pheasants roamed the fields like flocks of tame poultry, which in a way is exactly what they were.

Today's pheasant is on full alert. As you drive by on the tractor, their heads all go up. Those that are in the bottom of hedgerows scatter in panic as they seek to find a way through the hedge to safety. They know full well that whereas a few months ago the arrival of 'man' invariably meant more food, today it could be a signal that your backside is about to be peppered with shot. Especially if man turns up in numbers with spaniels and the like and you and your friends are encouraged to fly over men with guns. You also know that some of your friends and neighbours don't come back from this exercise.

Pheasants seem to take shooting in their stride better than partridge. Pheasants seem to settle back into their routine very quickly. They usually make their way back to where they were reared and continue feeding normally. True, they are on a very high alert status, but life goes on. Your partridge seems to me to be very different. True, there are far fewer of them but they always seem to live in clearly defined coveys within clearly defined territories. Often, I will disturb a covey in a particular place and know instinctively that that's the '15' covey, automatically count them and be correct. Shooting activity often breaks up a covey and drives them from their territory and, the day after the shoot, I often come across groups of partridge on the lanes and roads that seem totally disorientated and bewildered. Give them a couple of days and they seem to have settled down again.

I like partridge. I like to see them about, especially greys. I suppose this is another example of my species partiality. I also suppose that deep down I don't like to see them shot. I look forward to seeing them about with their young in the summer. But they do taste nice, don't they?

* * *

I WAS talking to a friend about harvests and combining in particular. Like most farming activities, there are anecdotes to remember. I was telling him about a contractor I once knew, who, at the completion of harvest, would park his combine in the middle of the yard and leave it there, out in all weathers, until just about a day before he needed it again.

The seeds would germinate and grow, cows would rub up against it, sheep would shelter underneath it and his poultry would explore its depths looking for grain.

When harvest-time came he would change the battery and fire it up, to see if it was all still working, once he had the threshing mechanism into gear.

I was there to witness this on one occasion. His hens had been laying inside all winter. Out of the back came dozens of smashed eggs and the foul smell was not far behind – among the debris of rotten eggs was the straw that had been used to make nests and two or three hens that had just had the fright of their lives.

* * *

ONE OF my granddaughter's pullets disappeared. I'd bought her three pullets and she had firm orders for 12 eggs a day from various teachers and family friends.

Just as they started to lay, one went missing. The family searched everywhere, to no avail. There was no sign of her, no feathers anywhere either as evidence of a visit from Mr Fox.

She phoned me up and said: 'If I lose any more of my chickens, my business will be in ruins.' This from a seven-year-old.

Then, lo and behold, as they say, or just like that, as Tommy Cooper used to say, the errant pullet returned, with no explanation, as though nothing had happened, and went on laying an egg a day.

Katie was at our kitchen table one day, telling the story to a friend of ours. 'Where do you think she went, Katie?' 'I just think she wanted to sample life on the wild side.' Walkabout, the Aborigines call it.

* * *

DRIVING ABOUT, on tractor or in Land Rover, the sudden movement of pheasants in fences and hedges is recorded in your mind subconsciously. Yesterday, something brown scuttling about in a fence caught my eye because its movement was different. It was a fox caught unawares by the approaching tractor. It's harvest time for foxes. Shoots go to great lengths to collect any birds that have been wounded. It's a part of shooting that is scrupulously observed but, inevitably, the odd bird is missed. Enter your fox to clear up.

I reported the sighting to the keeper who asked me the time of day I'd seen the fox and he was able to tell me, within about 30 yards, where I'd seen it. His knowledge of wildlife and its habits never ceases to amaze me. (Foxes, for reasons I don't understand, are called Charlies in this area. Hares are known as Sarahs.)

The keeper tells me that there are lots of 'new' foxes about. A keeper on a neighbouring shoot has shot 10 in the last week, all within half a mile of his house. Where they all come from bewilders me. When my children were young, my favourite TV programme *Bagpuss* sometimes used to show a chocolate biscuit factory that continually turned out biscuits but there was, in fact, only the one biscuit which a little rascal called Charlie mouse carried around the back of the factory in order that it could reappear in due course at the front. Foxes are a bit like those chocolate biscuits – they keep on appearing, endlessly. Where do they all come from?

* * *

THE WET and windy weather has seen the majority of our cattle into their winter quarters and the weekend work routine has become a full and demanding one. My son still plays rugby every week at a reasonably high local level. My wife reckons he's too old to be playing first team rugby, but when he started playing she reckoned he was too young so you can't win, as most men have discovered. Every Sunday morning she asks if he is all right from the previous day's game. Mostly he is, apart from a bruised this or that or a cut or a black eye. Last Sunday, he was completely unscathed.

On Sunday afternoon, he took his two boys ice-skating – a birthday treat – and broke his ankle badly. He must have been doing one of those triple whatsits but he hasn't told me how he did it yet. The boys will, when I see them.

What it does do is put a lot of extra work on the rest of us just when the routine workload reaches its highest. We're fairly pragmatic about injuries here and take them in our stride (is that a sort of pun?) For many years we were both playing rugby, and at one time I had a broken ankle and he had a broken arm. It worked out quite well in the end because I could do what he couldn't do and he could do what I couldn't do and we were both getting paid weekly by our private insurance policies. Come to think of it, that was about the last time we made any money. His mother says he will be off work for three months but I noticed this morning he had two sets of crutches – one for best and one for going around the cows.

* * *

NEXT WEEK we have our annual TB test. I'm dreading it. It will be four days' hard and difficult work at four different locations. In the summer it is a simple matter to move cattle about the fields so that they are handy to where we have our best handling facilities, but now they are all in their winter quarters we will need a bit of ingenuity and planning to achieve a test. Matters are not helped by having our main cattle handler immobilised while his leg is in a plaster cast. He has a particular knack of grabbing the unco-operative animals when they least suspect it and then has the strength to hold them while the vet does the test.

I'm also dreading the test itself. We haven't had a reactor for 20 or 30 years but bovine TB is rampant in this county. A herd a few miles away had 38 cows taken for slaughter a couple of weeks ago. The animals were on a large estate, not in any proximity to any other cattle, and they haven't bought stock in for years and years.

For farmers, it is quite clear that most of this infection comes from the reservoir of infection that exists in wildlife and in one particular species. It seems totally unfair to me that I have to offer up my stock for annual testing while the source of infection is not addressed. It is a question of balance that completely baffles me. It's OK for cows to be slaughtered but not the culprit. For farmers, it's a bit like trying to stop the tide coming in.

If we do fail our test next week, the restrictions that will be imposed on our business will be devastating. We could easily end up slaughtering calves at birth because we wouldn't be able to sell them at a month old, and we would have neither the room to accommodate them nor the food to feed them.

* * *

I HAVE ALWAYS, it seems, woken up at two or three o'clock in the morning. There is a very good reason why I wake up at that time these days, the details of which would be inappropriate to set down here.

Thirty years ago it would have been for a very different reason altogether but the details of that would be even more inappropriate.

This morning I was woken by a throbbing noise. As I lay in a semi-conscious state I, very feebly, tried to identify what it was.

I ran a sort of roll call of my body parts to see if all was well and decided that the only bit that was in any difficulty was my left arm. I was lying on it. The arm felt sort of dead and it was full of pins and needles so I decided that it was empty of blood and the throbbing noise was in fact the blood trying to get back in.

I turned over on to the other side and went back to sleep, pleased that I had solved the problem without having to wake up properly.

The noise woke me a second time but I drifted off again.

The third time I woke I turned over on to my back and I did another body check. After a few minutes, half awake, half dozing, I decided that the noise wasn't coming from me. I also decided to try to locate it.

First I checked my mobile phone. I use it as an alarm clock because I hate the noise it makes so it always does a good job of waking me up. I put my hand out in the dark and located the phone – it was fast asleep, just like I should have been.

I sat up in bed and realised the noise was quite clearly coming through the window. And there lay the answer – it was a rave.

They have one on a farm about three miles away several times a year and the drumbeat always wakes me up and invades my subconscious. I always wonder how loud it is if you are actually at the rave if I can hear it such a long way away.

I know the lad whose farm it was on; he's a grand lad, even if he is a bit unconventional for a farmer. I've asked him if I could go to one of his raves and he said I'd be very welcome.

I went back to sleep content and satisfied. For a few minutes there, I'd thought I was having one of my turns.

* * *

I'VE ALWAYS considered myself a dog person as opposed to a cat person. There are plenty of cats around our farm but I try to distance myself from them. To achieve this, I have always described them as feral, meaning wild, as in free spirits, free to come and go as they please. This is a particularly important distancing because my farm assurance says I should worm the cats. So, when the inspector asks me the appropriate question, I take him to a place where I know there are likely to be a dozen or so taking their ease. They bolt quite violently in all directions and I have proven my point.

But I give them milk every day and, for their part, they are expected to catch the solids in their diet. Every spring, they have lots of kittens which they secrete away in bales and the like, so that by the time I see them they are too big and too wild to catch. But there have been two litters born this autumn which is very unusual. Half of them are black, and half a beautiful grey colour. I have a dish hidden away behind some bales that I put nice, warm milk in twice a day, and hidden behind a pallet is a bag of cat food. The food isn't hidden from the cats but from the humans. The kittens get this food twice a day, as well as the milk, and now some of them will come quite close to me.

Don't tell anyone. It wouldn't suit my image, so let's keep it between ourselves. Men don't keep cats. They keep dogs, and real men keep working dogs. My dog is called Mert, an abbreviation of Mervyn who gave him to me. When he came here he had a name that was very, very politically incorrect so we quickly changed it to Mert. Mert is a real dog. In fact, he thinks he is a wolf. He probably gets that idea from watching our favourite film *Babe* too many times. Wolves like Mert prey on joggers, ramblers and cyclists. They are all legitimate quarry in his eyes, providing all the growling and aggressive posturing that can be done while he's in the Land Rover with me.

Outside, he's a bit of a pussycat. Mert had a brother called Neville who was renowned for being a bit on the nasty side, both in and out of a Land Rover. He would puncture the postman's tyres with ease, which wasn't much fun for the postman as he didn't dare get out to change the wheel. Neville was run over and killed last week (I don't think it was the postman). I haven't told Mert yet, as it would only upset him and he might decide to change his behaviour to that of his late brother in memory of him.

I once had a dog called Freddie, who was a spaniel and Jack Russell cross, which left him looking a bit like a small Basset hound. Freddie ran away with the gypsies. I fetched him back twice, but he was soon away again. Dairy farming has got to be at a very low ebb if your dog prefers to live with travelling folk. It was a blow to my self-esteem from which I have never recovered.

★ ★ ★

EVERY YEAR we buy straw from our neighbours for winter bedding for our cattle. We buy the straw by the acre, in the swath, after it has been combined. One neighbour grows a lot of cereals and every year he allocates us four or five fields, approximately, which is presumably as near as he can get to our requirements and the requirements of his other customers.

Every year we seem to get different fields, not that that makes any odds to us except, of course, that some fields are handier than others.

There's a main road through our village. I was giving directions by phone to a bed and breakfast guest on Saturday night and I told him 'keep following the main road'.

He said: 'I think I'm lost, this is hardly a main road.'

I said: 'It might not be a main road where you come from, but it's a main road around here.'

When he eventually arrived he said he'd called in at a pub a couple of miles away to ask directions.

'They didn't only know you, they gave me your number,' he said.

Anyway, that's a digression, back to the village and the straw.

At right angles to the 'main' road is a road that goes into the heart of the village. The village school is on the corner and the road is lined with houses, bungalows, picturesque cottages and there's a stream that runs the length of the village as well.

So, this year we were allocated a field of straw that can only be approached by this road. For how many hundreds of years have people been carting produce down this road out of this particular field? No idea, but what we are doing is hardly something new.

The people in the village can see the field, they can see there are still bales in it and they can see quite clearly what we are about. But every load we brought down the village was a real test of skill for the tractor driver as he ran the gauntlet of an obstacle course of parked cars and wheelie bins.

Of particular interest were the people who took their cars off their drive and parked them on the road to wash them while we were carting straw. There were wisps of straw in the air and some dust and as we snaked our loads tortuously past the cars, the hosepipes and the plastic buckets that were begrudgingly moved to one side, we had to wonder how their minds were working.

And as we drove on, I looked in the tractor wing mirror and could see Mr Indignant of Rose Cottage with his hands on his hips glaring at me before he flicked bits of dust and straw off his damp car. Not that this would always be a problem.

Come the era of food shortages, people won't be allowed to delay us like this.

Tractors carting anything to do with food production will have priority everywhere they go, and for jobs like these through villages, they will be fitted with snow-plough type devices and we'll be able to drive like bulldozers straight up the road, clearing the cars out of the way as we go.

* * *

SUNDAY MORNING, the cows have been milked and gone off to pasture, calves are all fed. Beans have been put on toast and consumed. The smoke alarm in the kitchen has had its daily test, courtesy of the toaster, and I'm back out scraping the muck up on the yards.

There are two cows shut in for the artificial inseminator and they are making a bit of a noise because they want to go down the field with their herd.

There are two inseminators who call here. There's a young one who farms as well and is often trying to sell me a bull, which, from his point of view, is a bit counter-productive. But it's the older one today. He's my age and supposed to be retired but he does 'days off'.

The day I started farming he came and signed me up for the AI service and he's been coming here ever since – 45 years.

You should always have time for people so I stopped the tractor and went for a chat. When he signed me up, most of the inseminations in this country were done by the Milk Marketing Board. It was a vastly different operation in those days. There were studs of bulls located conveniently around the country and semen was collected daily and served 'fresh'. Today it's all frozen and comes out of a flask in what they call straws.

We often reminisce, John and I (that's what older people do), and we often recall those early days of when he and I were young and fit. (He's still fit and has lasted better than me; perhaps he hasn't done as many miles as I have).

There used to be a system whereby you paid for the first service but any subsequent services on the same cow were free – presumably because it was assumed to be the fault of the bull or the inseminator if it didn't work. Which is a far cry from the world of today, where blame is always placed on the farmer.

Bulls and inseminators were assessed on what was called a non-return rate. I used to represent this area on an AI committee for North Wales. The best non-return rate in the UK was always at the centre in Dolgellau, where the bulls in use were mostly Welsh Black. You can see why if you look at their semen through a microscope. The sperm are big, bold, vigorous and with attitude. We still use Welsh Black semen on a cow difficult to get in calf.

At the other side of the village were a couple who milked three cows and one was difficult to get in calf. John went there every three weeks for three years before she conceived. That was a lot of free repeat services and cost for the price of one free service. No wonder the practice of free repeats didn't last.

* * *

I WAS WATCHING rugby on television, only I couldn't watch it as well as I would have liked because my glasses were filthy. My optician sold me a can of aerosol to clean them so I went to the kitchen to fetch it and a piece of kitchen wipe.

I tried to keep watching the rugby while I cleaned my glasses with the result that a casual squirt of the aerosol went full in my face and another squirt went all over me.

Half an hour later my eight-year-old granddaughter came in and gave me my customary kiss.

'You smell nice today,' she said, which made me wonder what I usually smelt like.

She's been too bright for some time.

* * *

WHATEVER HAPPENS from now on, this will be classified as one of the most difficult harvests ever. A reminder, if it were needed, that we take for granted our food supplies, anywhere in the world, at our peril.

Progress, when it eventually comes, will be very slow, with

combines having to tackle laid crops. Straw may be damp, soil will find its way into the combine and inevitably, from time to time, they will become blocked.

The threshing mechanism of a combine is towards the front and if a blockage occurs, bits of combine have to be removed and the blocked material dragged out, usually with difficulty, by hand. This is the conventional method but I once worked with a combine driver who could not resist climbing onto the back of the combine and disappearing into its bowels in search of the problem. I think he must have been a reincarnated mole because he would burrow away through the innards of the machine until you could hear him moving about quite close towards the front.

There were three of us on the outside one day and him on the inside when I motioned to my companions to be quiet and shouted out in my very loudest voice: 'OK, I think we've cleared it, start her up.' The cries of 'no' that came from the inside had us in stitches. There was a very fast exit from inside of the combine, head, elbows and knees were bruised and clothes were torn. Strangely, he didn't see the funny side.

* * *

I'VE NOT seen a rat about the yard here for months. This is good, very good. But it's not quite as good as you think. There is a price to pay for this rodent-free zone – a feline price; we are overrun with cats.

I don't know how many cats there are, they don't keep still long enough to count them. Could be 30, could be 50. Most of them are kittens.

They all live, not surprisingly, close to where we have calves on milk. Next to every calf pen there seems to be a receptacle that will hold about a litre of milk. Soft-hearted farmers are known to fill these with milk when they feed the calves.

We also have a very large bale of sweet-smelling hay. You probably don't need me to tell you this hay was made a couple of years ago. We put this sweet-smelling hay in nice little racks for the calves to eat. The sooner the calves start to eat some fibre, the better their digestion will work, and the better they will thrive.

Hay racks full of sweet-smelling hay, I have discovered, are ideal places for a cat to stretch out in comfort while it idles the day away until it's time for the calves to have some more milk. A nice little hay rack will hold three adult cats or about 10 little kittens.

Calves, I have also discovered, are less likely to eat hay if it's stinking of cats. Sometimes, on dark, wet days, my mind drifts towards the word 'cull'.

I know I could catch them and have them neutered but the last time I took about 20 of them to the vets, they got out of their boxes and nearly wrecked his surgery.

When he finally rounded them up, he pointed his finger at me and said: 'Don't you ever do that again.'

But I don't have only dark days, I sometimes have bright ones, and as I go towards the calf pens, buckets of milk in each hand, I have to smile at these semi-wild kittens that run to meet me, torn between their desire to be fed and their desire to remind me that they are indeed wild; backs arched, tails erect, spitting sparks, ready to fight me.

The dog keeps well away during these encounters. The dog, for his part, has developed a particular excitement on Friday mornings when I take the wheelie bin down to the bottom of the road. I suppose I have to pull it a couple of hundred yards and he becomes so animated about the process he has bitten me twice now. Only playful nips, but the nips are getting less playful as week by week the excitement mounts.

But I'll never swap him for anything. He thinks the world of me. He knows I'm in the house while I'm writing this and he keeps creeping further and further through the kitchen door.

I can hear the corgi, whose kitchen it is, growling at him. Now they are fighting and Mert is getting the blame and a bollocking to go with it. I'll take him for a ride in the Discovery in a minute; just the two of us together is the best company either of us ever gets.

★ ★ ★

I'VE GOT a friend who used to be a builder but did a bit of farming on the side. He took on some extra land one year and bought a lot more sheep. If you've got a lot of sheep, it stands to reason you need a good sheepdog. So off he went to buy one.

He went to one of those top trialists, who can make a dog do just about anything, and paid him £500 – which was a lot of money for a dog 10 years ago; it's a lot of money now.

We advised him, we in the pub, not to let the dog loose for a few days until it got used to him. He didn't listen and the next morning he went out into the field where the sheep were, made the dog sit down by his side, and then with all the panache of a contestant on *One Man and his Dog*, told the dog to 'Get by'. And the dog did get by, he ran around the flock of sheep in a perfect line beside the hedge, through the fence at the end and around the next field and the next and to cut a long story short, they never saw him again.

As far as I know, he could still be running – or then again, one of my friend's canny Welsh neighbours might have got himself a top-class dog, very cheap.

★ ★ ★

I HAD my day's shooting this week. Shooting is like a lot of outdoor activities: you have to have the right kit. By the time I started to get ready, time was already running out.

First off, the gun. I knew where the gun was – in the gun

cabinet, which is located well out of sight in an old attic.

The trouble with old attics is that there are lots of nooks and crannies in which to hide the key. As I hadn't used the gun for 12 months I couldn't remember which particular cranny held the key to the gun cabinet. It took me about 10 minutes with the torch to find the key. One of the few things that wind me up is being late so, as you can imagine, I was getting wound up by now.

The rest of the kit was no trouble; all I needed now were some sandwiches and a drink. Some sets have quite expensive bits and pieces to go with them, like stainless steel thermos flasks – one for soup, one for coffee – and nice little containers for food, with little compartments in them for whatever items happen to be on the menu.

My choice was between an empty ice-cream container and a plastic bag. I chose the latter. By the time I had emptied my wife's saucepan cupboard on to the floor looking for the flask, she was getting annoyed as well. 'You've left it outside somewhere,' she said. And I had, in a tractor cab. As I walked back to the house I gave it a bit of a shake to see if it was empty. The tinkling noise that came from inside told me that it chiefly contained broken glass.

The flask went into the black bin and I set off to shoot. My little plastic bag held one of those little drinks cartons with a straw fixed to the side that my wife buys for our grandchildren.

The first drive of the day reminded me that practice makes perfect and I needed lots of practice, because I didn't shoot a thing. After that my competitive streak kicked in, and I tried to work out what was going wrong and correct it. After three drives it was lunchtime, and I reckon I'd shot only four. But I didn't tell that to anyone.

Lunch took place around a table in a garage. My little plastic bag didn't look much in that company. All the others looked as if they had called into Harrods on the way, not only for the food they had with them, but for the containers they put it in, too.

Last to sit down is a farmer from Herefordshire. He farms in a very big way: there is a new four-wheel drive Mercedes outside. He had his lunch in a little plastic bag as well. I saw him looking at mine and our eyes met, and there's a flash of empathy and understanding there.

We had two drives after lunch, and on the first I was on the end and didn't get a shot.

Inevitably, my mind started to wander and reminisce about shooting, in particular the times when I used to do a lot more.

There was a gang of us in those days, who had played rugby together for years and we had taken on a fairly modest shoot. Boy, did we have some fun.

An important part of the fun was a spaniel I had that I had bought for £60, second-hand from a gamekeeper.

The dog's name was Bullet. We used to have an end-of-season shoot dinner, with awards in categories such as shot of the year, miss of the year and so on, traditionally presented in golden envelopes.

Bullet was always dog of the year but they wouldn't let him go to the dinner – I had to receive his prize on his behalf.

Lunchtime always made me think of Bullet, because we always used to stop for sandwiches in a tin shed in the middle of the shoot. One of my friends used to bring business clients to shoot, who we weren't allowed to make fun of. This was a bit of a struggle, but we didn't mind, because if he had clients with him, he would always pick up the tab for the bar meal we would have at the end of the day.

Anyway, during each shoot, we would sit down in this tin shed for our lunch. There would be various spaniels, Labradors and the odd sheepdog scattered about the floor, all of them except Bullet busy grooming themselves after their morning's exertions.

Bullet would sit centre-stage on full alert, apparently listening to our conversation. There would always be one guest who was there for the first time. These guests, given the types of people they were, would probably categorise themselves very highly, and would take it upon themselves to lead the conversation, mixing, as they were, with a group of 'simple farmers'.

Sometimes, eloquence in conversation is enhanced by the expansive gesture, the telling wave of the hand, and sometimes that hand might contain a sandwich or a piece of pork pie, or indeed, on the very first occasion this happened, a generous slice of camembert.

Bullet was, by now, facing the speaker. You wouldn't have seen him move; he must have just shuffled gradually until he'd turned around fully, without any of us noticing. Eventually, the piece of Camembert went just an inch too far. There was a blur of Bullet's head and we heard the click of his teeth.

'Your dog's taken my cheese!' the speaker shouted in surprise.

Everyone else was in stitches, and then the former owner of the cheese forgot what he was eating, and checked to see if his hand was still attached. Despite everything, he was fine. Bullet was not a dog to waste anything. I miss that dog still.

One day I received a phone call from a neighbour about a cow flat out with milk fever and, without thought, I jumped in the car and set off to attend her, forgetting that Bullet was loose in the yard. I didn't see him follow me to the end of the lane and under a lorry.

After this week's shoot we went to one of our local pubs for something to eat. I sometimes wonder if people think me aloof and unapproachable, because I often find myself on my own in company, just 'people-watching'.

That afternoon, there was a young lad doing the cooking. I

think he's between 16 and 18 years old, and he had a chef's outfit on. When he thought no one was watching, he fetched a half-pint glass, half filled it with one of those Irish cream liqueurs, and further fortified it with two shots of whisky.

This went down in two gulps and then he disappeared back to work. Fascinating.

* * *

I'M OFF to do one of my favourite jobs. I go on my own to do it, which is, in itself, a cause for some reflection – have I started to prefer my own company?

Most of the land I rent has, around it, what we call a six-metre margin. This margin is left to its own devices; it is left unfertilised, unsprayed and ungrazed. It forms what the 'experts' call a wildlife corridor.

Where we have, as we do in lots of cases, a six-metre margin in this field, a hedgerow, and then a six-metre margin in the adjoining field, it forms quite a considerable area of wildlife haven.

Add to this the several areas of cover that we grow, and it is no wonder that I can see a steady increase in wildlife. These areas are all receiving a payment which goes, in my case, to the landlord. I rent what's left in the middle of the field. The money comes from the funds that used to be focused on supporting the production of food and is now targeted at improving the environment which, politically, is more acceptable. Many people raise their eyebrows at the phenomenon, under a Labour Government, that sees huge quantities of money moved gradually away from the farmer to the landowner.

By midsummer, these margins are rough, overgrown areas. Now in their fourth year, weeds are starting to proliferate, and I see a problem here in the long term.

At the moment, thistles, docks and nettles predominate, but

there's a lot of ragwort appearing this year. My job today is to take tractor and trimmer and cut a strip around every margin. The strip is to be cut on the side nearest the field centre, and I think it's supposed to be an area where wildlife can dry out after a downpour. I'm supposed to cut it in July/August but I'm a bit late this year, but there's only you and I who know that.

I suppose what I like about it is the fact that it takes me slowly around the outside of every field and gives me a chance to take in every detail of crops, fences and wildlife.

The six-metre concept is probably the best value for money that anyone ever had. Farms and farmers are subject to random audits by Defra. These audits are at very short notice, I think 48 hours, and there is absolutely no chance of a postponement.

The audit may take up to three days and everything you do from field to livestock is put under the microscope. Defra has the ultimate sanction on all this because anything that falls short results in a reduction in your single farm payment. The width of six-metre margins are scrupulously checked and woe betide you if they are less.

That is why they represent good value for money because farmers and contractors alike err on the generous side so that my trip around the farm reveals that, in some cases, the margins are creeping out to eight or nine metres. I'm using this ride around to redefine the boundaries at the right width, but it's just a bit scary. Get it wrong and it could be like having your agricultural financial throat cut. Never mind all that, I drive boldly on.

I soon discover that our six-metre margin is where hares lie up in the daytime. Hares are starting to take over the world on my top ground and I hope that, when they do, they remember my kindly attitude to them. The keeper reckons there could be a hundred hares up on this hill, which would be a bit over the top because word could get around.

I hadn't known, until the keeper told me, that hares breed more than once in a season. I'd always thought it just happened in March. There's a hare in my silage field with quite small twins, which is something else I've not seen before. I wonder, as they scamper off, if they'll survive the winter.

There are buzzards everywhere and I see a pair of red kites every day. The leverets are in handy bite-sizes at the moment, a sort of 'leverets to go' on the menu.

* * *

AS USUAL I'm writing this in the kitchen in the early morning. It's quite peaceful and I can get on with the job in hand.

There's an occasional whimper from Mert, who sleeps in what we call the dairy. It's an old-fashioned back kitchen with slabs of stone where they presumably used to keep food cool years ago.

Mert is trying to get my attention so that I will let him out so we can go and look for adventures. It's a big step for Mert to come into the house at night. Neither he nor my wife know it's the first stop on a road that I hope will see him move into the kitchen. If I can crack that big step, who knows where he will end up - watching the telly in the sitting room?

We live in a fairly comfortable area with regard to crime; it's not that many years that we have been taking the keys out of vehicles at night. For some reason we still don't lock them although for most it's just a push on a button on the key fob.

Likewise we never lock the house doors at night, never thought to, never needed to, yet. But deep down I know it's a 'borrowed time' issue and we will eventually have to become more security conscious.

I suspect that it will be something like a break-in that will jog us out of our complacency. I have a theory that the casual thief will not bother to face an aggressive dog, he will just move on to somewhere a bit easier. If the thief is highly professional, he will cope with any sort of dog, probably in ways I wouldn't like to think about.

And if it's aggressive dogs you are looking for, Mert – he of the impatient whimper in the dairy – is just the man for the job. He's also very clean in his habits, which is an added bonus. Anyway, that's my plan but there's only us know about it.

Stretched out in front of the Rayburn is another dog. My wife's Corgi. He can be aggressive but he's far from it at the moment. He is a kitchen dog, he thinks it's his kitchen and his boundary is the kitchen door-step. If I'm in the house, Mert is always on the kitchen doorstep and on this threshold of respective territories, they have the most horrendous fights.

Every day there's the walking stiff-legged in circles and growling, and once a fortnight there's the fight. Mert always wins but it's the corgi that starts it all off, so he doesn't get much sympathy as he limps about for a couple of days.

Not until now that is, because the limping lasted a lot longer and the vet thinks he may have suffered an internal injury. He's on lots of tablets and feeling very sorry for himself.

Everything in life is relative and, about once a fortnight, we have to be extra vigilant in order to be on hand to stop a relatively nasty dogfight breaking out in our kitchen doorway.

I suppose we had allowed that diligence to falter just lately because our corgi, he of the kitchen territory, had been on medication to clear up a nasty abscess, which was the result of a previous fight. But, over the last 10 days, he had got much better and had returned to the aggressive patrols of his boundary.

Looking for a suitable metaphor, I would probably come up with sabre-rattling, that's almost exactly what he would do, make threatening noises on his boundary, provoke border skirmishes.

The situation is always made worse when I am away from home because my border collie Mert spends more and more time outside the door, impatiently waiting for me to appear. Recently, when I was away, a border skirmish turned into a full-blown international incident when, unfortunately, a very nasty dogfight was made worse when our bearded collie decided to join in on Mert's side.

This intervention on Mert's side tipped the balance and the fight progressed into the kitchen and, I am told, there was blood 'everywhere'. Today, I am alone in the kitchen, Mert is in his usual place on the doorstep and the corgi is on a drip down at the vet's, badly beaten up. We'll have to resolve this somehow.

It is usually customary for dogfights to finish quite abruptly when one dog rolls on his back to signify submission. This is not on the agenda for our corgi which came to us out of Ceredigion, was Welsh-speaking when he came here, and for whom rolling over is simply not an option. Currently England rugby players will be familiar with this phenomenon.

An innocent inquiry of my wife that Mert should be allowed to sleep in the kitchen while the corgi was at the vet's met with an outburst that left me reeling, given that I have come from such a gentle background.

For some time I have been looking for a good home for the bearded collie who does nothing much except eat, sleep and chase cats (recently I caught him trying to climb up on the bird table).

He is at the time of year and at the stage of coat growth when he closely resembles a Herdwick sheep and he will probably be easier to re-home after his annual clip. Not many people are looking for a sheep to sleep in their kitchen.

* * *

IT'S A FUNNY thing, territory. I remember many years ago we went out for Sunday lunch to some friends' house. My son David was about three or four years old. These friends kept bantam chickens. 'Would David like a cock and hen for pets?' It seemed like a fairly innocent gift. No big deal, we let them loose on the yard and away they went.

Twelve months later I did a head count and we had 73 bantams. They were highly prolific because if you found a nest and took the eggs to eat, which was the idea, they would immediately lay somewhere else and you couldn't always find the new nest until the chicks appeared.

These 73 bantams split into clearly defined gangs. There was the stack yard gang, the cattle shed gang, the workshop gang, and so on. Just like our dogs, there would be horrific fights in the gateways that seemed to define their territories; there would be blood and feathers everywhere. Most of them were caught and sold or given away. Foxes accounted for the ones I couldn't catch.

* * *

LAST AUTUMN we upgraded a tractor. The finances of dairy farmers are in such a parlous state that swapping a 25-year-old tractor to one half its age is a big deal. I would have liked to have kept the old tractor but couldn't afford to do the deal without the £5,000 it was worth as part exchange. Ever since we did the deal I have felt guilty. We'd had that tractor about 15 years; it had been a good and faithful servant, and I miss it.

Sometimes I go up to the yard to do some task or other and find myself looking for it. I did make tentative inquiries of the dealer who bought it about its whereabouts. 'It's been exported to Greece.' Greece! What sort of life will it have there? What sort of home has it gone to? I feel really guilty; no proper goodbye, no proper thank you, no gold watch.

* * *

WHEN our cows are feeding in a long row there's about a 2ft space behind them and the adjacent wall.

When I walk this space, as I often do, I am always conscious of a pressure at the back of my legs, which is Mert, keeping close behind me. I know the cows don't mind me walking close behind them but I'm not sure about the dog.

This confined space is a very good place to get kicked; the kick would be aimed at the dog but he's so close to my heels there is no doubt at all that I would have to share it with him. But I could turn this to my advantage.

When I take Mert out and about I always leave him shut in the Discovery because not only does he have a fondness for nipping cows' ankles, he will bite any other ankle as well.

I quite fancy taking him out of the Discovery and letting him meet our public. I wouldn't put him on a lead, there is no dignity in a lead for a dog like Mert but, if he keeps as close to my heels as he does around the yard, I should be able to control him.

Top of my agenda is the big poodle that lives in the shop where I get my papers. This poodle, fully trimmed up in proper poodle fashion, is a bit full of himself. I bet he's never met a dog like Mert and I know for certain that Mert has never seen anything like it.

Could be an interesting meeting. Could it be time for the poodle to find out a bit about the real world?

* * *

FOR SOME TIME I've been concerned about my diet. I'm not concerned about dieting, I've been doing that for years, to little avail. My first cup of tea of the day, in which I allow myself a spoonful of sugar, is a daily treat, the prospect of which will get me out of bed on many a dark, wet morning.

It's the implications of our bed and breakfast business on my diet that concerns me. Most of our guests spend weekends with us, which means that, on Fridays, my wife does what she calls 'a big shop'. As this shopping is put away I receive very clear warnings:

'Don't eat these, they're for the guests.'

At particular issue are fruit and yoghurts, both of which I enjoy. So every week I have a fruit-free, yoghurt-free weekend. For breakfast, our guests have a large bowl of fruit and a wide choice of yoghurts. Come Monday, it's a different story: 'That fruit needs eating up,' says my wife.

I ascribe to the five-a-day theory, but on some days I am expected to eat 10 or 12. Yoghurts are a different story; every week I not only consume yoghurt that has gone past its sell-by date, but push the boundaries on those dates way beyond recognised limits – and I'm still here to tell the tale.

* * *

LAST SATURDAY I was grumpy. Very, very grumpy. We have this machine, you see, still fairly new, that we call a straw chopper.

Simplistically, you put a great big bale of straw in the back and it chops it up and blows it some distance to where it makes a nice even bed for cattle to lie on.

But it wouldn't work a week ago, so we sent it in to the supplier where it spent three days and was returned fixed and ready for work.

I put it on the tractor on Saturday morning and it still wouldn't work. So I drove it six miles for the dealer to have another look and, after two hours, he once again declared it to be OK. The trouble was that we couldn't really try it out on his yard because there was a large bale in the back with its strings removed. Not only would his yard have been full of chopped straw but just over the fence is a business that transports new cars and all their lorries were packed full – we suspected that they wouldn't welcome the new cars being covered with straw and, besides which, a bale usually contains the odd stone.

So, I drove back home to try it again and it still didn't work. My less than gentle sarcasm on the mobile brought the dealer out but to no avail and we ended up emptying the straw by hand. He went off promising to return on Monday morning, my son had gone off to play rugby, it was lunchtime (what lunchtime?) and I still had about three hours' work to do before milking.

So I set off with the dog to look at the cattle that were still out, my grumpiness close to being quite nasty. But it was such a nice day I couldn't keep it up for long.

In the mile-and-a-half I have to travel to our other ground, I passed three different shooting parties. When I got to the little valley where my dry cows are they were just shooting that particular drive. I switched off the engine to watch – it would be bad manners to drive between the guns and the beaters but, even more important, not safe.

It was a spectacular drive, the birds flying out of the acre of maize that I allowed the keepers to grow on one of my fields, back across to the woods they think of as home.

The drive finished and I drove slowly on to see my cows. I had the windows down and all the beaters said 'hello', some of the guns waved as I went by, and some of them called out 'All right, Rog'. But some of the guns ignored me; too up themselves by far. I came across the one who runs the shoot and stopped to say hello.

He was ecstatic about the drive they had just had. I let him dig himself a hole and then I said that if it was such a good drive I'll want £1,000 next year if I am to allow them to grow another game crop. His face was a picture and he laughed nervously at my joke. The grumpiness may have gone, but I was still not in a good mood. A couple of hundred yards further on, I met my friend the keeper, a transformation in his posh shooting outfit – he usually goes around disguised as an urban guerrilla.

In the mirror I saw him watching me go, thinking about it. I bet I could get a bit more money out of them when the time comes.

A couple of hours later and I was making a similar journey to put out bales of silage for the cattle still out. There was only one shoot still active, it was plenty late enough in the day; pheasants need some time, after being so violently disturbed, to get their bearings and to find somewhere safe to roost.

There were small groups of pheasants everywhere, on full alert, some standing in the middle of fields they'd not been in before, some scurrying down lanes trying to find their way back home. Lots of pheasants in lots of places where you would not normally expect to find pheasants so near to dusk.

* * *

SO I'M getting on the train again to go to London, to Westminster, this time as part of a presentation to MPs of the wide range of dairy products available in the UK dairy industry and the innovation that is going on all the time to produce new lines.

This is a very important occasion for me, as no-one from our village has ever been to London twice in one year. I remember about 20 years ago organising a trip from the pub to the Smithfield show at Earls Court. Seventeen of us went and only two of us had ever been to London before, but that's another very long story.

So I get on the train, which is very full, and the only seat I can find is next to a young girl, probably in her late teens. Well, it's only half a seat really, because she's asleep with her head against the window, her coat as a pillow and her bum half across the seat I paid for.

Anyway, I squeeze in as best I can and, about 20 minutes later, we stop at a station and this disturbs her.

She wriggles about a bit trying to get comfortable, gathers

her coat up, folds it into a better pillow shape, plonks it on my shoulder, reverses her position and goes back to sleep couched up next to me.

I don't mind really, she's a very pretty girl, but doesn't need those piercings.

The train pulls into Euston; she wakes up, stretches, gives me the sweetest of smiles and says 'thank you very much'. And off we both go wherever our lives will take us, the only evidence of our meeting some make-up and a whiff of perfume on my shoulder.

As usual I had no breakfast so I go to one of those fast-food outlets which purports to be French but which is always staffed by Asians and East Europeans and order a latte (keep the milk sales up) and a cheese croissant (very sophisticated) and sit at a little table on my own to watch the world go by.

'Is anyone sitting there?' asks a very smart lady of about my own age. This is another big event in my day; no one usually wants to sit by me.

I think I dress about right for my age, go with the flow – you can't stop life's clock. She's putting up a bit of a fight – she's trying to look 15 years younger. She's very elegant, although the elegance is fading a bit.

She's got coffee and a croissant as well but she's finished before me. She gets a tissue out and dabs around her mouth and discards it. Then she gets another tissue out, takes out her top set, wipes it clean, applies some adhesive and pops it back in again.

I'm too fascinated by this to pretend I'm not watching, but she just gives me a smile and goes on her way. That's two smiles already this morning and it's not 11am yet.

* * *

THIS MORNING I went for my pre-operation check-up, before surgery on my bad knee. I'm sure I've told you about my bad knee. I've told everyone else.

For people-watchers like me, there are rich pickings to be had in hospital waiting rooms. I'm very early for my appointment but the waiting room is almost full, probably because everyone except me seems to have someone with them. There are about four different people to see in this procedure, and I'd been sitting there only a couple of minutes when my name was called.

Lots of questions here. Have you had this and have you got that and I'm soon back in the waiting room. But only for another couple of minutes, because I'm called again.

This time it's blood pressure and ECG and stuff like that. Finally, the nurse says she's going to take a swab of my nasal passages. 'What for?'

'To check to see if you have MRSA.'

My alert antennae are on full stretch now. 'Do you have MRSA in this hospital?'

'No, and we intend to keep it that way.'

So she pokes this long cotton bud thing up each nostril and then she says: 'I can't believe you've done that.'

I think: 'What have I done now?'

She goes on: 'I've been doing the MRSA testing in this hospital for five years now and up until you, every single person that I've approached with a nasal swab has opened their mouth.'

She obviously thinks that I'm a bit special now, which is something my mother and I have always known.

Back in the waiting room and the original whispered conversation between companions (which are, of course, a British tradition) have developed into full-blown conversations with fellow patients, with such lines as:

'Where do you come from? Oh really! Do you know so-and-so?'

Two down and two to go. I reckon I'll be out of here soon;

then I see a notice that says pre-op checks can take up to four hours!

A man comes in on his own; he's carrying a briefcase-sized box. The front of the box is transparent and you can see that it is subdivided inside into 12 compartments. The sort of thing that I would keep electric drill bits in if I could find any.

A hush goes over the waiting room as the spectators take in all this medication – there's pills in every compartment. This must be a proper patient, really ill. Apart from being about five stones overweight he looks as fit as a fiddle to me.

I'm sitting there for two hours now. 'Doctor's delayed in the wards' they say; that's fair enough, no problem to me.

This is a renowned orthopaedic hospital and some of the things you see here really put life into perspective.

There's much to-ing and fro-ing of the other patients, though, and as each successive couple is called, there are cries of 'good luck', and when they come back they are greeted like heroes.

People are also whispering to their companions and then slipping away on their own to do the 'sample'. They think I can't see the sample pot hidden in their hands. Mine is empty in the breast pocket of my shirt and, at the moment, I've never felt less like a pee in my life.

It's my final call to the surgeon, and we have a look at my X-rays. 'Mine used to be like that,' he says, and we spend 10 minutes talking about rugby.

That's it then, only the urine sample now. It's a bit of a struggle and I soon get it over with.

When I come out, all the nurses are having a bit of a gossip and I am introduced as 'the one who knew his nose wasn't in his mouth'. It's a job to squeeze past the waiting room door as people say farewell to those they've known only a few hours. I can see that a lot enjoy the attention and are almost loathe to go home.

Me, I can't wait for the operation, full fitness again and going back to being bionic.

★ ★ ★

THERE'S A HILL near here that is something of a local landmark. If you lived on the plains of Cheshire or the wetlands of Somerset you might call it a mountain but everything in life is relative, and around here it's called a hill.

It's a big old hill mind, goes about 10 miles down. Most of it is owned by the National Trust and it provides common grazing for the farms that adjoin it. The people who make a living off it, with their natural this and natural that, project this and project that, outnumber the farmers and very probably their sheep by some distance.

There are lots of sheep on the hill; I've seen grouse on there, hardly any cattle and a few ponies, although there used to be lots.

I'm never really sure what these various bodies are looking for in their ideal of vegetation on the hill.

We read a lot about 'overgrazing' that will 'spoil' everything but what is there now is the result of what has gone on before, in the way of livestock, so it doesn't really tie in.

But then if you earn your living running a project that is running a hill and you say everything is OK, well you don't need the project, do you?

Hill-sheep production used to be subsidised on a headage basis, so the more sheep you had, the more subsidy you got. That's all stopped now and farmers are paid a lump sum based on what they received historically, so there are nowhere near as many sheep on the hills today.

I read somewhere that there are now four million less sheep in Wales, for example, than just a few years ago.

* * *

IN THE SUMMER, at weekends, the sound of motorbikes intrudes on the peace of early mornings. Almost everywhere we go in the country these days we are implored to 'think bike', as we drive about.

But unfortunately, the bikers themselves don't seem to read these notices, because our local newspaper always has reports of accidents and deaths over the previous weekend.

Yesterday there was a new sound, gunfire, marking, or at least reminding me, that shooting started at the beginning of September for partridge and duck.

However, the natural world that I see every day is slowly being taken over by the pheasant. In just a few weeks, they have transformed themselves from the shadowy shy birds that hung around the release pens, to getting larger and bolder and now they can be seen everywhere.

Their comeuppance, gunfire, will start in November. It is ironic that when I note these preludes to the shooting season that I have just seen a hen pheasant with a nice brood of poults, and a partridge with a hatch of chicks. If they've got any sense, and they probably haven't, they'll leave off learning to fly for six months or so.

One day I saw five red kites on one field. I don't know if kites have a collective noun to go with them but it was a nice sight.

What had brought them there I don't know – perhaps they were a family on some sort of outing.

Out there in the media world that knows more about nature than those of us that live amongst it, they have just woken up to the fact that your average badger is very partial to a hedgehog supper. I've only seen one hedgehog run over on the road this year but lots of badgers.

I've been looking out for hedgehogs on purpose and I drive a lot of miles. The run-over hedgehog used to be almost a given on any journey and the disappearance of the one and the proliferation of the other is a clear indication of the populations of both species.

It is also a given that farmers are bracketed in with badgers, for destroying the hedgehog habitat, which is a shame because they probably have more habitat than they've ever had for a generation. Two metres are now left untouched around every field, six metres around lots. Am I expecting too much in hoping that the 'experts' will finally wake up to the fact that badgers also decimate the nests of ground-nesting birds?

A quite reasonable and probably justified law to curb the activities of badger baiters has inadvertently let the badger population get out of control with a negative effect on other birds and animals.

* * *

THESE DAYS, when I get in to the car to go off somewhere, there's something of the airline pilot, pre-flight check about my preparations.

Firstly, I have to get my phone to connect to the hands-free kit fixed to the sun visor. Sometimes it connects first time but mostly, it doesn't. There's quite a lot of buttons to press and I don't always get it right.

Next is the sat-nav. I don't usually need this until the last few miles of my journey and that's only if it's a new destination but it's still a bit of a novelty so I switch it on.

I'm used to women telling me what to do. I suppose it's something of a comfort zone. I've chosen an Irish female voice. I've always been a bit of a soft touch for softly spoken Irish women. I was deeply in love with that woman, I think she was called Assumpta, who kept the pub in Ballykissangel.

I suppose it was just a crush, an infatuation, and as we get older we learn that we have to shrug these things off and move on with our lives, but for a time it was a very real love and very important to me. I think I was in my late 50s at the time. I used to fantasise about going to live with her in her pub and enjoying the party in the bar.

I'd probably have a couple of cows in the field behind the pub that I would milk by hand so that she always had some nice fresh milk to put on her cornflakes in the morning and if we had spare milk I would make it into cream to put in to our Gaelic coffee night caps just before we went up.

Enough of that, I can fantasise about that when I'm stuck on a tractor all day.

Anyway, the first time my wife comes with me in the car when I have the sat-nav working and she hears the first instruction 'turn left in 400 yards,' she snaps at me: 'I suppose you chose that voice to remind you of that damned barmaid in Ballykissangel!' Can a man have no secrets?

* * *

IN A PREVIOUS life it is highly possible that I was a buzzard. There is an undeniable logic to this.

To all of us who observe what goes on about us in nature it is quite clear that crows hate buzzards. From dawn to dusk they harass and torment them and, as the buzzard moves from area to area, there are always 'fresh' crows waiting to take up the challenge.

So, when a particular buzzard eventually dies and is reincarnated as a farmer, namely me, the persecution goes on.

I have come to this conclusion quite easily; today we have completed the planting of about 60 acres of winter wheat.

From the vantage point of my high ground there are freshly

drilled fields as far as the eye can see. Everywhere I look, tractors are ploughing, working down and drilling.

We farmers are ploughing the fields and scattering the good seed on the ground as never before. Could it be something to do with wheat prices at record levels?

On all of those fields there is already an opportunity of a harvest for the birds. Worms, grubs, spilt seed, easy pickings, full stomachs. And where are all the birds? The ground is black with crows.

There is a feeling of persecution about it, much as a buzzard is persecuted throughout its life.

* * *

MOST OF my life, no that's wrong, almost all of my life, has involved getting up early in the morning. There's no genetic reason why dairy farmers should be able to cope with less sleep than everyone else but we do and, invariably, we are always tired.

Sometimes there's an opportunity to 'top up': wet lunchtimes at weekends, for example. Just half an hour can be a real help. But woe betide anyone who wakes you up during that half-hour. Children for miles around go about on tiptoe while I have my snooze. Last Saturday, I had just closed the second eyelid when I was disturbed by a knock on the door. I had been woken up by a young van driver.

Showing amazing restraint, I listened while he told me his story, which brings me to another pet hate of mine: the proliferation of road signs in rural areas. Some villages have about eight signs at each end to tell you that you are approaching a 30mph limit. We have an unclassified council road through our farm, most of it impassable except by tractor or 4x4. But a few years ago, the council put a sign at the other end indicating it as passable. There is a no-through road bit incorporated in the sign but it doesn't tell you where the bit is that you can't get through.

Two years ago, a big articulated lorry tried to get through and we had to cut half a tree down to allow it to pass, there was no way he could back up one and a half miles on a narrow track through a steep field. This was my van driver's problem. His sat-nav didn't know little local details like that either, and he had gone off the road and become stuck. It was amazing that he hadn't turned his van over.

I took him back in the Discovery but that wouldn't look at it and it took an hour to pull him out with a tractor. I don't think he could believe that we didn't try to touch him for £20 for our trouble, but it wasn't his fault. I've never had a problem with giving people a helping hand.

* * *

IF YOU TALK to people who are involved in animal welfare organisations they are always eager to see the number of journeys that animals actually have to make kept to a minimum. They will cite stress and the possibility of injury as good reasons why this should be so. We have to transport animals most weeks as they make the journey between our two areas of land.

The cows, for example, are well used to going off for their 'holiday' when they are not milking and stroll into the trailer quite readily. When it's time to bring them back we can usually load them easily in the corner of a field somewhere. Part of making sure that they don't injure themselves is to drive very gently round corners and when we stop and start. Inevitably, this causes a queue of traffic to build up behind you that usually includes some very aggressive, impatient drivers. So we become quite unpopular and, because of this, we very rarely move cattle on the road on foot, but two weeks ago we had to.

We had a group of 22 cows in a field. Two of them had calved and five others needed to come home. As this was quite a big 'sort-out' we walked them down the road to a neighbour's yard where we could manage the job a lot easier. There were two calves, two mothers and 20 doting 'aunties', so progress was fairly slow as each cow in turn took the opportunity to eat some of the roadside grass before dashing back to check on the welfare of the calves.

After 100 yards we acquired a car following us. It was a narrow lane, two cars can't pass on it without getting on the verge, but nevertheless he made several attempts to try to pass us, eventually giving up and turning round and roaring off the way he had come. It's one of the downsides to being a farmer as you go about your business: if you put cattle in a trailer it's wrong; if you move cattle on the road it's wrong.

People have been moving cattle on roads for hundreds of years; you would think that by now we would have established some sort of right. If you are patient, and occasionally I am, life will reward you, because half an hour later when we were returning the 15 cows we didn't need to their field, who should get stuck behind us, but the impatient driver of earlier on? He stuck it out this time and as the cattle turned into their field I gave a very friendly wave and 'thank-you'. I'm no lip-reader but I've got a good idea what he said. I won't share it with you because I know you are all much too nice to upset by profanity.

* * *

FUNNY THINGS peacocks; who would think such a beautiful bird could make such an awful noise? We used to keep them and I could never get over how hardy they were. Percy and his pea-wives used to live about 30ft up in a tree next to the house. It can be no mean feat to hang on to a branch all night, with about 6ft of tail hanging down behind you.

You'd have to roost facing the wind, that's for sure.

The strange thing was that if we had a bad spell of snowy weather, Percy and his wives would transfer to the small henhouse we had.

They might sleep there for several days if it was really cold and windy, but one night you'd go to shut the hens up and the peacocks wouldn't be there, they'd be back up their tree. Sure enough, next day a thaw would have set in: how did they know that? I miss Percy, but I don't miss the terrible noise he would make if someone put a light on in the night to go to the bathroom. We do farmhouse bed and breakfast here and you'd hear guests say: 'Oh look at that beautiful peacock.' Next day, you'd hear them say, angrily: 'Did you hear that peacock in the night?'

* * *

OVER THE last few weeks, thousands and thousands of sheep have moved homes about the country. Autumn is the time of year when, traditionally, young yearling ewes, bred to produce future lambs, would move from the upland areas to better land in lowland areas to produce prime lambs for the table. It has always been good practice to go to higher land to buy your ewe replacements so we have had our hill ewes, wherever they lived, crossed with rams of a lowland breed to produce a ewe that would produce a good crop of lambs. It is all quite simple. The hill ewe would usually produce just one lamb, but because that lamb had a lowland father it would hopefully produce lots of twins. I think there are more than 30 native breeds in the UK, so there are a huge range of crosses available and within that, crosses within crosses.

There are fashions in sheep as well. Forty years ago, the two most popular breeding ewes came from the Welsh borders. They happened to be pure breeds, the Clun Forest and the Kerry Hill. Both breeds would come close to the rare breed category today. I always thought the Kerry to be a particularly attractive sheep with its white face and distinctive black nose. The Clun has a woolly head and legs, loathed by some shearers because they take longer to shear and for which they may charge an extra 50p.

There's something compelling about sheep. There is huge pride in ownership and visits to the great sheep sales can be compulsive. When I kept sheep I would often get a phone call to say: 'I was thinking of going to such and such sheep sale. Do you fancy coming for a ride?' You bet I did, and off we would go, not intending to buy anything, but we often did. A local friend of mine used to breed Welsh half-breeds, which were the result of a cross between a Border Leicester (a white-faced sheep with a Roman nose) on his Welsh mountain ewes. It used to be a big important day in his farming year, particularly from a financial point of view. A few of us would go to 'help' him and inevitably we would end up in the market bar. If there had been a good trade there would often be some singing going on by 5 o'clock.

Sheep sale anecdotes are endless. The same friend and I went in his car one Saturday to a small local sheep sale where he encouraged me to buy three Suffolk ram lambs because they were cheap. He also had no problem with putting them in the back of his car to get them home.

'It isn't far, they won't have time to make a mess', but they did, and when we let them out of the back door of his Cortina ten minutes later he didn't think it was such a good idea.

Another friend of mine decided he wanted to try a bunch of ewes called Llanwenogs, native to West Wales. There were five of us in the car and, as we got nearer to the sale, the friend who wanted the ewes confessed that he had always envied the aura of the big sheep buyers who came to our own area and today's journey was the closest he would ever get to that.

In order to look the part we had to stop at a garage to buy him some cigars. When we got to the sale, he went first to the auctioneers and told them he was looking to buy a lot of sheep that day (he actually wanted 20-30) and would there be enough lorries available to take them home? The auctioneers made frantic phone calls to local hauliers while he leaned on their office counter and puffed nonchalantly on his cigar. Then we went to see the sheep. There were thousands there, but we couldn't find any Llanewenogs. In the end we had to ask.

'There aren't any here today, their big sale is next week.'

It was a disappointment, it was an open-air market, it was pouring with rain and by 11am we were in the pub. We spent several hours in there, stopped in a couple on the way home and got back to our local by 10 o'clock. We were thrown out by a quarter past 10 and that was as close as any of us actually got to buying that particular breed of sheep. Next morning, while milking, I wondered how many hauliers actually turned up looking for these so-called big sheep buyers that were in the area.

Winter

LAST YEAR, a lady arrived here in a new Audi to stay for a couple of nights' bed and breakfast. She was immaculately turned out – smart suit, new hair-do, perfect make-up. Not all, in itself, that remarkable, except that she was in her mid-80s. I thought at the time: if that's growing old, I'll have some of that.

What had brought her to our front door was the fact that she was researching her family tree, and she had discovered that her ancestors had lived in this area in the 1500s and, in fact, some of them had lived and farmed on this farm. She had a copy of the family tree with her, a huge piece of research, about three pieces of A3, and for 200 years her relatives had lived, worked and bred in this area.

People obviously didn't travel as far to meet people in those days – no foreign holidays to meet people from wherever, no favourite daughters going a couple of hundred miles to university and coming back with a scruffy, layabout boyfriend who lived a couple of hundred miles in the opposite direction (who, in stories with happy endings, probably smartened himself up eventually, got a good job and proved to be a good husband and father – I like stories to have happy endings).

What was particularly remarkable was the fact that one of her relatives who lived on this farm had successfully reared 16 children, because all of their marriages were chronicled as well.

Last week, two brothers turned up here to stay who were on the same quest. They had the same surname as last year's lady but didn't know of her. For people researching their history, as they were, the copy of last year's family tree, which she had left, was like winning the lottery. They had with them a map of our farm dated 1820 which we had not seen before, a copy of which we now have and which we will duly frame.

The fields are largely unchanged but bear names, some of which we use today, and some I've not heard of. I'm very tempted to try to reintroduce the old names as substitutes for what we use now. How long that would take I don't know. Upper and lower cow pasture sounds better than roadside field, but disappointingly, in some cases – six, in fact – the fields are just called by their acreages. Contrary to the widespread views held of farmers, we actually have more fields now than when we came here, on the same acreage, because I split one very large field into three. In 40-odd years I've never pushed a hedge out and I've only cut down one live tree, and that was because it was so close to the house I couldn't get any insurance.

The lady who came last year even had the farming diary of her ancestor. It was quite clear from that, that in the order of things as they were at the time, the last thing to be was a 'day labourer'. Day labourer must have been another description for peasant. Horses apparently came higher up the social scale of the time. For example, Captain pulled the mower all day in the Great Clover Piece, but a day labourer, who apparently didn't have a name, cleared the ditch around New Leasowes.

IT'S HALF past four on a Saturday morning. The milking machine pump has been going for 10 minutes now. Calves are being fed, some by torchlight. The old tractor that goes around the buildings twice a day gathering up all the 'number twos' that the cows have done in the night has coughed into life. It stands there in tickover mode still coughing and belching, wreaths of blue smoke spread through the shed. It's a bit like an old man having his first cigarette of the day. It's a scene you would find on our farm every morning in the winter, only the activity would be nearer to five o'clock.

This morning there's a bit of urgency about everything. The two of us are going out for the day. We've about four hours work to do apiece before we go but on our way home tonight, we'll probably think we've had a day off.

Tomorrow morning it will be business as usual, but the 'day off' will have left us tired. When I was young, people used to tell me that you didn't need as much sleep as you grew older. It was a lie.

* * *

THE LOCAL population of wild turkeys is growing. 'My' keeper had four of these North American turkeys on the shoot. Well, there's a quiet lane that I take to get into town that passes another keeper's cottage that is on the side of the lane.

He's got three of these turkeys, a stag and two hens, and they are mostly to be found in the lane itself. It's no good being in a hurry because as soon as the stag sees a vehicle coming he takes up a position in the middle of the road and starts his display. I drive right up to him but he doesn't move.

He goes out of sight in front of the truck and I can hear him pecking away at the bumper. As his hens move on down the grass verge, he follows slowly and I can hear him as he pecks his way down the side of my vehicle. I don't move on until I can see him in the side mirrors and I know that he is safely past me.

To celebrate his triumph over this vehicular intruder into his territory, he usually mates with one or other of the hens. There's not much chatting up involved, no foreplay that I can detect, and the hen doesn't seem particularly distracted by the process.

Definitely a quickie.

* * *

WILDLIFE usually keeps its heads down in bad weather.

But this December, strangely enough, with plenty of bad weather about, there seems to be more activity than usual. I've seen hares about a lot more, and I hadn't seen one for over a month.

One day, the fields were alive with fieldfares. There were thousands of them for about five days and then, just as suddenly, they were gone. I tell the keeper about them but inevitably he already knows and inevitably he's always got a better story to tell.

He tells me that while out feeding early one morning in the dark, he put his lamp across a field and counted 62 woodcock out feeding. He reckons they feed out on the fields at night and go back into the woods in the daytime. Personally, I think 62 woodcock would take a bit of counting in the dark but I don't question it.

I was always disappointed at how eager shooters were to bring down a woodcock and could never really understand the need to shoot such a lovely bird when there were already plenty of pheasants to shoot – now I hear of more and more shoots that leave woodcock alone.

The poor things have come a long way to get here, and they deserve a rest and some safety.

NEXT to one of my silage clamps is a patch of briars, about 20 yards by 20, and the briars are well established, offering plenty of cover.

It must be a warm, dry spot because most days there's a large covey of partridge in there. I tell the keeper about them. 'There should be 30 in that covey,' he says.

As we all know by now, the keeper is big on counting things, although how he counts them goodness only knows. When I drive past in the truck they explode out of the briar patch like shrapnel from a hand grenade, and are impossible for me to count anyway. Still, he's not to know that. 'There were 31 there this morning,' I reply, 'they flew down into the wood.'

He thanks me for the information. I've no idea where they flew, I wasn't watching, but he's not to know that, either.

* * *

I'VE JUST spent ten minutes watching the goldfish. On a scale of sadness that comes up as quite sad, but for me, at least, I found it quite interesting.

He, she, or whatever, was moved from a long rectangular concrete cattle drinking trough to a round plastic one and I took the time and trouble to teach him to swim in circles after he had spent most of his life swimming lengths. The boys had wanted to move him back to where he was, but there's more activity around the round trough and I think he enjoys it. He's quite a fine fish, probably nine inches long, and the first thing I noticed during my observation was that when a cow goes to drink, he swims right up to the cow's muzzle.

The cows usually go to drink just after they've been feeding and there are always some particles of food clinging to the hairs and whiskers around the muzzle. While she is drinking, the goldfish carefully picks this debris off to eat, even lifting his little head an inch or so out of the water for a particularly tasty morsel.

The cows that use this particular drinking trough are what we call our high-yielders. The diet that the fish shares with them is very high-calorie stuff, and I expect to see an increase in his size in a very short time. But there is a darker side to this goldfish (I can feel a name coming on for him, but I'm not quite there yet). Part of the moulding of this plastic tank includes the recess where the ballcock sits. It's set into the side of the tank where cows can't rub it off. The plastic balls that float up and down, regulating the water level, are bright orange. Goldfish are bright orange as well. So where does our fish spend his time when he's not feeding off cows' muzzles? Rubbing himself up and down against this orange ball.

I can only assume that he has fallen in love with it. This has got to be a cry for help and next time I am in town I will get him a companion from a pet shop. This fish came from the fair, but I don't think he should have to wait until May for the fair to turn up for a real companion.

I'll be doing him a favour and I'll probably be doing the new fish a favour as well. While I'm at it, I might as well buy three, one for the round trough for company and two for the long concrete trough, and then all the cows will be clean around the muzzle.

★ ★ ★

HERE WE go again. A new year, a new A4 pad, same old fountain pen, same old kitchen. It is inevitable that I write reflectively on what has happened recently.

Well, Christmas happened. To start with, I was asked to do one of the readings at the carol service in our local church. This was a surprise request for me, and a surprise for quite a lot in the congregation, too.

There were seven readings and it was a bit like the Royal Command Performance when you wondered who would be on next, as various readers made their way to the front to do their turn.

After, we had mulled wine in one of the side chapels and several people came up and said they were surprised to see me there and surprised that I'd done a reading. Whether they were surprised at my presence or that I could read, I'm not sure.

The next night was Christmas Eve so I went to the pub for an hour. It's strange, but no one said they were surprised to see me there.

The tanker driver gets a full English breakfast on Christmas day but this year he was haunted by the sight of a man and a little girl walking through a town centre at four o'clock in the morning. It troubled us both and the only comfort we took was that he was holding her hand and she seemed quite content. It's the world we live in sadly. And it is sad.

It was my intention to just stay for an hour but we all know what happens to intentions. I knew I had passed the point of no return when I asked someone for a half-pint of mild and they bought me a large scotch.

One thing about our local, you can always find someone to drive you home. A young girl in her early 50s drove me home in my car and I was home by midnight, which was just as well as it's up again at a quarter to four as the milk tanker is here just after six.

⋆ ⋆ ⋆

MOST OF my sheep-keeping neighbours have been scanning their flocks recently. It's a process where a contractor comes and produces a scan that determines how many lambs each ewe is carrying.

This is very useful management information as the flock can be subsequently divided up into groups that are carrying singles, twins, triplets or are actually barren.

Lots of farmers let the ewes with a single lamb out of doors where they can protect just the one lamb from the weather and predators.

A friend of mine was so pleased with the results of the scan he showed me the printout in the pub. He's a bit of a local legend; got sheep everywhere and no-one knows exactly how many. I didn't look at the results of the scanning, as I was busy adding up the numbers of his various flocks.

'Always wondered how many sheep you had,' I said. The piece of paper was snatched away with such force I had to check my fingers.

* * *

TODAY WE will consider, if you will, public conveniences. And in particular, gentlemen's public conveniences. They are a facility in which I take a special interest, as I will explain later.

Last week I had occasion to use the gentlemen's facility in our local cattle market, which is provided by the local authority. I knew that these toilets had been refurbished recently but had not yet taken advantage of them.

What a revelation, without going into particular detail; they were a celebration of stainless steel. It was everywhere. There were places to wash and dry hands and somewhere in the background there was classical music, it sounded a bit 'tinny' but then I suppose with all that tin, it would, wouldn't it?

I was disappointed with the hand-driers, to which I pay particular attention, as they were located in a sort of recess in the wall.

Let me explain. Many years ago I found myself spending the evening in licensed premises. There was nothing remarkable about that, but what was remarkable was the weather. It was January and we were in the middle of a spell of freezing fog. It was a raw, damp cold that chilled your very bones – not weather to linger in.

I got into conversation with a local character, a young man given to spending his time in hostelries as well. Such was his consumption of alcohol that one of our local doctors bet him £20 he wouldn't live to see 40. On the day of the appropriate birthday he made an appointment at the doctor's, waited his turn, and duly drew the £20, which he had converted into drink and consumed by lunchtime.

To return to our story, he told me that for reasons associated with excessive drinking, he found himself homeless and had slept the last three nights on the steps of the cattle market and was shortly to spend the night there again.

I was appalled, given the weather as I described, that a young local man should find himself thus. I took him home with me and made him a bed in the attic above our kitchen.

I had him out from there early next morning and he actually spent three nights there without my wife knowing. By then I had bought him a caravan, we moved him in and he lived there for 12 years, after which time I found him a council flat.

It was a roller coaster ride of 12 years. There would be a job for a few weeks, an accumulation of some money, a two-week binge, no job, no money, a few odd jobs in return for some food and away we would go again on the same cycle. But there was an unexpected bonus. Everything in life is relative and, in comparison to his lifestyle, my own seemed relatively sensible. For a time, my wife sensed that she had married a relative paragon of virtue.

The link between gentlemen's conveniences and this latter story? I've always been interested in other people and how they live their lives. This was the only person I ever knew who had found themselves homeless, so I was always interested in the detail.

'You should always,' I was told, 'seek out a toilet with a push-button hand drier.' These buttons come in two sorts, one can be wedged into place with a coin, the other needs some sticky tape to hold it in. Having done this, the warm hand-drier will run all night and the homeless person can curl up on the floor underneath.

I always find myself checking this detail – you never know when you might slip through life's safety net and be in need of this skill. The hand-driers in the new toilets cannot be used in this way, located as they are in a recess in the wall. I thought this to be inconsiderate.

* * *

I USED to have a Transit van and there was a spider living behind the rear-view mirror that was fixed on the outside of the driver's door.

We drove thousands of miles together, the spider and I, and I often used to wonder what he was thinking about as we drove along.

In hard times, I used to catch him flies and put them in his web. He used to scuttle out and drag them back behind the mirror. I always thought he was grateful for that.

When I sold the van, I tried to catch him so I could transfer him to the next van, but he wasn't having any of that.

When I sold that van, I was given £1,000 cash and a cheque for £400 – drawn on a bank account that had been closed for a couple of years, so I'm £400 and a spider light on that deal.

As that took place about 10 years ago, I don't hold out much hope of ever seeing either again.

I miss the spider more than the money.

* * *

THE RECENT cold dry spell has allowed us to spread chicken muck on the 100 acres of grassland that provide our first-cut silage.

A dry spell is essential if we are to avoid tractors damaging the grassland, which is a pet hate of mine.

Chicken muck is a wonderful manure and used regularly it raises worm populations considerably, improving soil condition remarkably. It has the added bonus that it contains the grit that was fed to the chickens, so we are topping up the calcium at the same time.

Before we had poultry we would put five hundredweight of fertiliser on our first cut silage ground, now we put poultry manure plus just one hundredweight. On 100 acres, that means we reduce our fertiliser use by... I'll let you work that out for yourselves, you can do that instead of the crossword. Some time soon I will take the chain harrows over it, just to spread it about a bit better, plus the mole hills, and then put some nice stripes on it with the roller. You can smell the chicken muck for 24 hours after it's spread, but its all part of life's rich pattern.

I was feeding the dry cows with silage soon after we'd done the muck-spreading and I could see two ramblers hesitating on their journey. As I drove home they were still there – it's at a place where they often seem to lose their way. The path is rarely used so there is no clearly defined way and the next stile is out of sight down in a dingle.

'Is this your field?'

'Yes.'

'Why have you removed the stile?'

'I haven't, it's down there by that black and white cottage'.

This is win-win stuff. They quite obviously have enjoyed taking the opportunity to take me to task and I in turn have taken some pleasure in pointing out that they are at fault with their map-reading and not me with my farming.

So, the atmosphere quickly turns to be quite friendly and we exchange pleasantries about the weather and the view.

'Your silage has a strong smell to it this morning.'

I think they are referring to the silage I have just fed the dry cows. I sniff the air, but couldn't smell it, but then I'm used to it.

'Sticks to your boots.'

I look down at their feet and see traces of chicken muck stuck around their boots from crossing the grass fields where we were spreading it yesterday.

'It does, doesn't it?'

And on they go. If they are happy thinking they've got silage on their boots, who am I to tell them what it really is!

* * *

I RECENTLY popped my head through the door of the hairdressers and quipped: 'Any chance of a quickie?' (The old jokes are always the best.)

There were a lot of women in there – it must have been a Friday, though I'm not really sure.

There's a lot of sexism in a ladies' hairdressers. Various ladies take it in turns to go behind a curtain across the end of the room. I can see a couch in there but little else.

The curtains are put very carefully back into place after each client so I can't see what is going on, but I note that I never get invited in. My haircut took about five minutes and cost £5 and a lot of banter, (my vet charges a pound a minute as well and I ponder on that).

I was quite disappointed when it was finished and readily accepted the cup of coffee that's offered. There were four women sitting in a row in a sort of halfway stage in the hairdressing process – they all have silver foil randomly arranged in their hair.

They listened, fascinated, to the conversation between me and the girl who owns the shop: our talk was, at the same time, both risqué and flirtatious.

As she was about 30 years younger than me I suspect it does more for my ego than hers.

'How come,' I asked, 'I never have that silver stuff in my hair when I have my hair done like all these others?'

'No need for it, there's plenty of silver in your hair already.' she replied. Thank you very much.

THERE'S been a lot in the media this week about milk prices. A leading UK banker told me last summer that 30 per cent of his dairy farming clients were actively looking for a way to leave the industry.

Last week at a conference in London, a leading European banker told us that at current milk prices, anyone who had invested in dairying recently was very vulnerable.

As the production of the 50 per cent who have left dairying in the last eight years has been largely taken up by people who have invested in expansion, we could have a situation where more than half the dairy farmers remaining could leave quite quickly.

There's plenty of money between farm gate and the supermarket checkout, it's just not shared out equally.

We don't produce nuts and bolts, we can't switch on and off at will. When you switch cows off, they usually end up in an abattoir.

* * *

WE HAD a big day out in Cardiff for the rugby. The final of the Six Nations Championship is as big as it gets – especially when there's a Triple Crown, Grand Slam and Championship title on the line.

The tension was building up nicely – and it had plenty of time to because it was a 5.30pm kick-off. But we all tried to make the best of it.

I always go to the same bar, always drink red wine and always have the same meal – I'm set in my ways.

Lots of people I know came to the bar that day and as I was to find out to my cost later in the day, too many of them bought me a drink.

But there were also opportunities to be had. All the women that came up to my table to say hello seem to want to be kissed, some of them several times, so I had to go along with that.

But the surgeon who did my knee operation last year was also present and he came across to say hello. I reminded him I had an appointment to see him in a couple of weeks' time, when he would decide whether to do the other knee.

I told him that the other knee seemed fine now that the knee that was operated on is back doing its fair share of the work. So we decided, he down on one knee by my side, and me sitting on a chair (chairs being very precious and vacated at your peril) that we would cancel the appointment for now and if the knee becomes a problem, he will put me back in to the system. I quite liked having a professional consultation amid all the noise, drinking and excitement that was going on around us.

Many years ago there was a dentist in this area who would go around the pubs quite a lot in the evenings, and he would pull teeth in the pub should the occasion demand it.

Payment for this service would be part-cash, part-drink, and I suppose that in some way it was a sort of predecessor of the supermarket home-delivery service, only years before its time.

Anecdotes about this dentist were abundant. I remember one story of the farmer who had a really bad tooth but was much too busy to leave harvest to have it attended to. So the dentist was summoned to the harvest field.

The most convenient place to perform the operation was to lie him on the bed of the binder they were using (I told you it was many years ago!) Trouble was, the anaesthetic didn't work very well and the dentist only had enough for one injection with him.

So the poor old farmer was lying on his back on the canvas of the binder with the dentist and various helpers sitting on him to hold him down while the tooth was removed. They reckoned that you could see the bloodstains going round on the canvas for two or three harvests before they were worn away. I just love these sorts of stories; they are a part of rural folklore.

When I first came to live in this area I was young and fit enough not to have much need for doctors and dentists but inevitably, in time, I needed a dentist, and had no hesitation in deciding to go to the dentist I've mentioned. 'You can't go to him,' says my wife, 'nobody goes to him.' But I did – I knew where he lived and so I just went and knocked on his door. There was no answer at the front so I went around the back. I knocked on the door and a voice told me to come in.

He was sitting there at his breakfast, and I told him I thought I needed a tooth removing. He paused with a piece of toast half way to his mouth and his expression said 'Me?' as though he was astonished at my request.

If he was astonished, he was also delighted. 'How did you know about me?' he asked. 'Someone told me you were a very good dentist.' And he glowed with happiness.

He took me upstairs to a bedroom which was his surgery. The first thing that struck me was that the dentist's chair had a certain age to it; the second thing that struck me was that the floor was littered with dental paraphernalia, most of which was false teeth.

Without seeming to pause he made his way to the chair, one leg seeming to do all the walking while the other made sweeping motions as it cleared a path through the debris for me to make my way to the chair.

The syringe for the anaesthetic was also old, older than anything we used on the farm, and stuck a bit. I wondered for a moment if he would have to apply WD40 to lubricate it.

But he took the tooth out skilfully without much trouble and I made my way home none the worse for the experience.

We were out that evening and my wife was telling everyone that I'd had a tooth out that day; they didn't show any real interest until she told them where I went.

Everyone was amazed. 'But no one goes to him,' they said. And for a couple of hours, well, I was something of a hero.

* * *

I'M WRITING this on Sunday morning. The milking is nearly finished and I've snuck into the house for another cup of tea. My demeanour this morning is best described as disconsolate. If I had to put it to music, it would be called *'The Pissed-off Dairy Farmer Blues'*.

I switch on the television and the main news item this morning tells the story of a hard-drive containing the personal details of prison officers. It has been lost, or stolen. You'd have to have a pretty sad life to want to read that on a Sunday morning. Now, if it were the bank statements of some of my neighbours, that would be very different.

Yesterday afternoon, before I went out to milk, I checked our 'close to calving' cows. They are put in a shed for the purpose, with plenty of room and plenty of nice clean straw – the bovine equivalent of having a baby with BUPA.

Two of our best cows have calved since this morning, unaided, obviously without too much difficulty, and now the calves are up suckling their dams. They are by a dairy bull and are beautifully marked.

I didn't go any closer until this morning and, as I approached the calves, I thought they would make really smart cows. But they won't, ever, because they are bull calves and have no sale value whatsoever.

But that is not the real loss. We aspire to have a healthy herd of cows that are all home-bred, self-contained and not exposed to any disease risks that might arise from bought-in stock. To do that, we need to have about 40 heifers coming into the herd every year. For the second year running, we look like getting only 20.

Nature usually sends a 50/50 split of heifers and bulls and we ensure we always have at least 90 cows in calf to the dairy bull to achieve our target.

As nature is still probably sending along the equal-sex split, who, I ask myself, is having all my heifers?

OUR VILLAGE blacksmith passed away a couple of years ago. He lived to a good age and in his latter years he only did a bit of pottering about, which was fair enough.

But you did see the door to his small shed open, so that you knew he was about. His blacksmith's shop has stood empty and quiet now for those two years but recently it has been sold with planning permission to convert to a dwelling.

It is the start of these new works, fencing a garden in and altering the access, that has a finality about it that is, in a way, more eloquent of the end of an era than his passing away.

They were never very auspicious premises, the first part where he kept most of his equipment, just about large enough to take a small car but that led in to the forge proper which was a treasure trove of forge, bellows and traditional blacksmith's kit that was a joy to see.

All that, they tell me, is still there and supposedly there is a condition of planning permission that it must remain so. It would be a devil to dust! It would be far better to put it somewhere where everyone could see it on a regular basis.

It's the passing of an institution. Years ago it was an important meeting place where you met your neighbours while you waited your turn to have something made or mended.

We would all contribute to the job at hand, with advice or actually assisting in the mending, if it was harvest machinery that needed mending urgently.

Employees would enjoy the social side of the visit and employers would get tetchy about how long they were there.

There was always an unspoken rule that you could jump the queue if your job was urgent and depended on the weather.

Our late blacksmith's great skill was in wrought iron work and I know of several great country houses where his gates grace an impressive entrance.

I often wondered what he thought about having this great skill, yet spending most of his life looking in the scrap pile in the nettles for a piece of broken sheep hurdle to mend someone's mower.

When I first came to live around here there were two blacksmiths, father and son. Father was in his 70s and thought they should make their living shoeing horses. Son wanted to make gates and mend farm machinery and there was great competition between them. It could be quite scary at times.

If there was a horse to be shod, equipment had to be fixed outside, even if it was pouring with rain. All that wet and all that electricity made me twitchy, but it wasn't that much safer inside in the dry, with the old man fixing a shoe front end of a horse and all those sparks flying about at its back end.

The father (sounds better than old man) was a great prankster and would love to tease serious horse owners, especially if they were a bit on the novice side.

One day he had me holding a horse's head while he trimmed its feet prior to shoeing. It was a young lady's first horse and the first time she had had it shod. She watched what went on, wide-eyed and fascinated. He did all four feet and then stepped back to have a look.

'Do you think the horse is level now, Roger?'

I gave the halter to the owner and joined him to eye the horse up.

'I think it's a bit high on that one corner.'

So he lifted the one hoof up and took just a token sliver of hoof off. We stepped back and had another look.

Just to be sure I fetched the spirit level and we did several checks with it on the animal's back before we were satisfied. By now the owner's jaw was well dropped, but she never said a word.

The new shoes were duly fixed but there was more to come. The owner had ridden the horse to the blacksmith's and the saddle had been removed for shoeing.

So Father Blacksmith enquired of the owner which way she intended to ride home. He went to great lengths to determine that she was going to return the way she came and not take a ride around the village first.

Having determined that she was going back the way she came he picked up the saddle and put it back on the horse, facing the wrong way round. He explained that this would save her turning the horse around.

His parting shot was to enquire, indicating his son welding outside, if she wanted to buy some sparks to make her own Christmas decorations. An old blacksmith's joke, but always amusing the first time you hear it.

* * *

THERE was a time when I was given to drinking on licensed premises on Saturday nights. There was a group of us who would congregate in the same pub, in a particular area of that pub, where we were all sitting in close accord on three sides of a small bar.

It used to be quite a competitive issue, laying claim to this bar area, because there was another group that used to seek it out as well.

They used to irritate us because they used to smoke what we called 'funny fags' and would take up valuable, and coveted, bar space for the whole evening while only drinking a couple of halves of mild, their relaxation coming from whatever they were inserting into their rolling fags.

Ours was a good crowd of real country people, farmers, farm workers, and some who didn't work on the land, but came from a rural background; for example, lorry drivers who would help you shear or cart bales at weekends. The landlord would sometimes put a 78 wind-up gramophone on the bar and we would end up with a singsong.

It all disappeared when the pub closed for a couple of years and we all went in different directions on Saturday nights.

What I took for granted at the time and which also disappeared was a lift home. For years I would pick up a neighbour and drive him in the four miles to our local town and at 11 o'clock, as good as gold, his wife would take us home.

Drinking and driving was strictly a no-go area around here at the time. We were possessed of a very driven local policeman who had a mission in life to clear the roads of cars. He would lurk about on the outskirts of the town while the two local 'specials' would watch pub car parks and radio him when a prospect left to go home.

Not for a minute am I condoning drinking and driving, but he would breathalyse people sleeping in cars. He got my son while he was relieving himself against a barn wall as he set off to walk home one night, just because he had his keys in his pocket.

He would breathalyse farmers in the early hours as they drove in Land Rovers to go around their sheep at lambing time.

A lift home was very precious and still is.

Times change and we all move on, but sometimes I do fancy a visit to the pub on Saturday night. If I've been away a lot during the week I'm not bothered, but now I occasionally go to the pub in the village.

It's only a mile-and-a-half away and, in theory, I reckon I'm safe to drink four halves, but I've usually drunk them by nine o'clock. It's not far and the roads around here are very quiet and the incentives to have 'just one more' are very tempting.

I don't think I'm much of a danger on a road where I am unlikely to meet more than one car; it just needs a bit of common sense, because the same rules apply to me as those to someone driving at 70mph down a motorway.

Going back to the times when we had that good crowd together, central to our fun was a great character, now sadly departed, who farmed in the hills outside town. He would be in the pub by seven o'clock every night of the week and taken there by his wife who would fetch him home at 11pm.

His vulnerable time was lunchtime at weekends when he would drive in for a few pints on his own. The vigilant policeman referred to earlier, started to take interest and actually chased him home a couple of times, but didn't quite catch him.

My friend, a resourceful man, made a plan. For most of us the plan would have involved staying at home at lunchtime, but he had other ideas. Halfway home for him, down these narrow lanes, was a sharp 90-degree bend. There was a gateway on the angle of the bend and inside the gateway, but also at an angle, was a large barn.

The theory was that if he thought the police car was after him, he would drive straight through the gate and take a right-angle turn at speed into the barn and be out of sight, where he thought he would lie low until he decided it safe to go home.

He even practised this manoeuvre a couple of times to perfect it. I came upon him one Saturday evening in the pub in reflective mood. We were on our own and I could sense something had gone wrong: 'That Lewis, the policeman, was after me at dinnertime.' There's a long pause now while he tends to the need of his pipe. It's up to me to drive the conversation on.

'Did he catch you?'

'No, I've been ready for him for some time.' He gets quite animated now as he tells me the story. 'You know that sharp corner by Davies's barn, well I've had my eye on that for some time. I went straight through the gateway at about 30mph and whipped round into the barn and out of sight. About a minute later Lewis came roaring up the road, blue lights a-flashing, never saw me. He went back 10 minutes later and I walked home across the fields.'

He puffs on his pipe and takes about half a pint out of his glass.

'Well that's all right then,' I say, 'you got away with that.'

'No it's not, they'd parked a bloody baler just inside the shed and I drove straight into it and wrote my car off.'

His cars were never very valuable; probably third-party, fire and theft, so there would be financial loss to undermine the moral victory. 'He thinks he's going to take my licence off me, but he never will.' 'Why not?' 'Never had one.'

* * *

MANY YEARS ago, I used to breed Labrador pups. I had one bitch to start with, and over a short time the vets gave me two more that had been left at the surgery to be put down.

We used to get a similar phenomenon to the handbag scenario. This was explained to me by a friend of mine: if a woman gets out of the car with her handbag, she's come to buy. If she leaves the bag in the car, she's just making an enquiry.

When I had a litter ready, Mum, Dad and kids would turn up to see the pups. The children would soon be knee-deep in adorable yellow or black Labrador pups. All that was missing to complete the scene was unravelling toilet rolls. 'How much did you want for them?' the woman usually asked. 'We haven't decided yet if we'll have one or not.'

'I bet you haven't,' I'd think. 'I'd just like to see you go away from here with those children without a puppy.'

The last time I deliberately bred a litter of pups it was out of a most remarkable border collie bitch I had. She was the best working dog I ever had (it's OK, Mert won't know I said this, he's not big on reading and writing) and I thought I would breed a bitch out of her in the hope that mother would teach daughter in her ways of working. So we chose a good working dog and, in due course, a litter of pups turned up. I chose a bitch that I would keep and advertised the rest for sale.

Our local daily paper comes out early afternoon onwards depending on how far you live from the head office. The first purchaser was on the yard at 3.30pm, a very attractive young lady wearing a very smart business suit. She took the jacket off to reveal one of those very pretty white blouses that ladies sometimes wear that is see-through enough for you to see what very pretty lingerie they have underneath. I don't tell you this to titillate, just to complete the picture.

The pups were in a shed and she asked for them to be let out so she could see them better. Farmyards can get muddy. One after the other, she picked the pups up to hug them to her bosom. Should she have a dog or a bitch? One or two? As she deliberated, others turned up and bought pups, and after two to three hours she had to settle for the only pup left.

You should have seen the state of her.

* * *

THERE is a part of my life that finds me speaking after dinners. It's not something that I ever sought to start with; it's just something that sort of crept up on me.

For many years I organised our rugby club dinners, including the speakers. There were countless rugby internationals with just a handful of caps who would want thousands of pounds to come to your dinner. I thought 'I'll have some of that' and for a time, indeed, I did charge a fee.

But the agricultural community has its feet very firmly on the ground and will not pay anything like that amount for a speaker. I would ask for a fee that, per hour away from home, wasn't much at all, to be met by the response: '*How much?*'

You'd be surprised how many people expect you to drive 200 miles for nothing.

Could it be that the dial on the petrol pump goes around so fast these days you can't see the figures anyway, so they think it's for nothing.

These days I confine my after-dinner activities to requests from my friends or members of the dairy co-operative I am involved with, so don't construe what has gone before as some sort of advertisement for more appearances.

What I do now is ask for a donation to the NSPCC, which is a bit close to my heart because I think children are so special and some have no chance at all in life.

I had to speak at a friend's birthday party last Saturday (and very generous he was, too, to the children) and while I spend some time thinking about what I am going to say, I have a habit of making my notes at the last minute which, if something goes wrong, can make me a bit tetchy, and infuriates my family.

Last Saturday, I chose the hour between the end of milking and time of departure for this very important part of my preparation. I laid out pens, cue cards, started to write and the electric went off. The rest of my preparations were done by candlelight and torchlight.

Sometimes I go to a dinner and can't remember what I've written; this time I couldn't see what I'd written, either. A candle, I discovered, is not that handy in a shower.

Showering, shaving and dressing in the dark were not easy so, when I eventually got to the dinner, I was pleased to see that I had the right suit trousers on with the right jacket and most of my three-day beard had gone, though there was still a lot more on one side than on the other.

You never really know how a speech will go, it's all part of a sort of masochism that drives you to do it in the first place, but I thought it all went really well considering the indifferent start to the evening and I drove home well pleased with myself.

It was a late night and an hour less in bed next morning but I've learned to take that all in my stride and, I suppose, as I went about my work next morning I was still rather a bit full of myself.

In particular, I was thinking about the story told to me by the lady sitting by me at the dinner that night who worked in a local town's bridal shop and had sold a wedding dress to a 57-year-old man that week – for his own use.

Before I let the cows go down the fields to graze, I had to sort a cow out for artificial insemination.

When cows are in season they exhibit a sort of nymphomania with their herd mates. Sometimes they can be quite shy and it takes some spotting; sometimes it is at the other end of the scale and is shamelessly blatant and boisterous.

This cow, one of the biggest we've got, was well in the latter category. I knew I would need to hold her back with a companion to keep her company, but that wasn't good enough, she wanted to stay with the whole herd. Three times I tried to drive her in to the holding pen; three times she got past me.

The fourth time I tried I was wholly concentrated, thoughts of last night's dinner were well gone, it was time to test wills and determination. I got her on her own and reopened the pen gate.

The cow had two choices, through the gate into the pen or through me. She went through me with some ease, not so much brushed me aside as sent me flying. I tried to break my fall on to the concrete with some sort of a roll which served only to make sure I had a more comprehensive covering of the three-inch deep brown stuff that I was now lying in.

As I lay there, feeling the cold wet seep into my clothing, I fleetingly had to acknowledge that when I stood up I would present a very different spectacle to the one a few hours earlier entertaining at a Saturday night dinner.

At the fifth attempt to sort out this cow, cold, wet, filthy beyond belief and not without quite a few bruises, I felt fully entitled to search for a stick. The cow could see the stick in my hand and allowed herself to be sorted as good as gold.

My mistake was that the slurry on my trousers has the chance to run down to my socks inside my wellies which, until then, had been the only dry bits I had.

Anyone arriving at our back door over the next hour would have been greeted with a pile of filthy clothes topped with my best boxers.

'You didn't strip off outside the door!' scolded my wife.

I suspect I would have been in a lot more trouble if I'd stripped off in the kitchen. She put the clothes in the wheelbarrow and threw some buckets of water on them and left them for Monday morning.

* * *

SOMEWHERE at the back of my mind lurks the vague memory that someone, probably going right back to an old music hall song, used to sing words to the effect that there were '40,000 feathers on a thrush'.

If I've imagined it then I've probably got a bit more of a problem than I thought. If it were true, then how many of my precious brain cells have I tied up remembering that?

Whether there are, in fact, that many feathers on a thrush I've no idea, but I do know that there are also a lot of feathers on a pigeon. The evidence of that is here in the grass before me, where something has made a meal of a pigeon.

There are feathers everywhere. I'm left with the thought that it must be a very sharp fox or cat that can actually catch a pigeon. Over the next week I find about a dozen dead pigeons, which seems quite remarkable. I ask the young lad who drives the tractor for us and he says he's seen a lot as well.

He's in love at the moment and has a job to find the tractor some mornings, so if he's seen a dead pigeon it's even more remarkable. I start to see odd pigeons standing about on the road that look really sick so I begin to suspect they have a disease problem. I prefer not to contemplate that it is bird flu but the next time I find a dead one I stop to examine it. It's plump, so it can't have been that sick, well not for very long, anyway. I pull some feathers off and find an oldish wound that looks as though it were caused by an airgun pellet.

Presumably someone, somewhere, has a kitchen garden that is suffering from the depredations of pigeons and is defending his crop with an airgun. It just seems a pity that he (or she) doesn't get a better airgun, one that will kill the bird outright rather than condemn them to the slow, lingering deaths that I have been witnessing.

I haven't seen one of the 'second crop' leverets for three weeks now. I'm a bit disappointed as I have been looking for them and as I also said, there is less cover for them now so they should be easier to spot.

On Saturday mornings the keeper is always busy about the shoot and so I ask him. He says that foxes have had them all and that he hasn't seen any either. He goes on to say that there are three 'new' foxes on the estate and in his words they are 'lamp shy'. This means he's been out at night with a powerful lamp and rifle but that the foxes won't stand and look at him. If they do he will see two reflective red eyes and that, as they say, will be that.

Keepers are always busy at night with lamps seeking to reduce the large numbers of foxes that are about, and I suppose that disturbed foxes will move to other areas, thus the description 'new foxes'. Shame about the leverets, though. I'm showing partiality to species again. This will almost certainly become politically incorrect with the passage of time. How long before a wild boar or a wolf released into the wild ('because wolves are a native species') kills a child? How long before a town fox kills a child? Not that long, I suspect.

* * *

I AM convinced that the world as we know it will slowly but surely come grinding to a halt. Not because of global warming, not because the fuels we presently use will have run out, not because of pestilence and disease and not because of nuclear war.

It will be because of a lack of common sense and too much risk assessment. I used to be very involved in our village school but your children grow up and your own life moves on. There used to be two arrangements in place at the school that benefited the wider community. For decades the children made their way up the village about 150 yards to the village hall to eat their lunch. The road they walked is unclassified; the only real traffic on it is traffic to and from houses within the village. There was an extra bonus because the village hall benefited in the form of revenue so it was the sort of commonsense, win–win arrangement that worked all round.

A risk assessment on the dangers of the walk itself has stopped the practice and the children now remain in school for their lunch.

Fifty yards away from the school in another direction is the school playing field, it's not big, it's of primary school proportion, but it's got goal posts and you can have a decent game of football there. And for generations that's what the youth and children of the village have done. (Played football there myself.) But that's been stopped as well. If someone were injured there out of school hours, would the school be held responsible? Of course they would, in the sort of society we live in today. But children will be children, and children will continue to play football, so where do they play football now? On the main road through the village of course. Wouldn't you know it, it all defies belief and leaves people of my generation lost for words, words that you could print anyway.

* * *

TO MY great delight there are a group of seven curlews to be seen in the area. They cover quite a large range but turn up on my ground several times a week and will, I hope, become a regular feature in my life, most especially to hear their call.

I've seen four lapwings making a fuss of just one chick. So at the end of term let's hear it for the curlews, well done, 10 out of 10. Lapwings, you will have to do better.

THE STRONGEST relationship on this farm is, by some distance, me and the dog. He idolises me; in my shadow, always there for me, the one I can confide in and trust.

But like any honest relationship, there are areas where we struggle – the main one is when I have to go on a tractor, because he wants to come with me.

When I get on the tractor he's tight behind me, poised to jump up into the cab. If I'm not going far, or for long, then he often joins me. But if I'm going off to do a job that will take a few hours, it's not that handy.

The only place for him to lie on most tractors is down on the floor on the right hand side, and if he curls himself up, that's fine. But after a time he often wants to give himself a bit of a stretch, and that in itself is quite reasonable.

The trouble is, he's lying on the foot throttle. It can be quite disconcerting if I'm approaching a hedgerow and looking out of the back window at the implement I'm using and Mert decides to shift himself to a more comfortable position, which includes lying across the throttle, so without any warning I find myself travelling at twice the speed I was into a fence or hedge.

Harsh words have been exchanged on these occasions and the dog, without any knowledge of what he has done wrong, gives me a crestfallen look that breaks my heart and makes me feel guilty for the rest of the day.

I don't like fall-outs, especially with the dog, so when I went off on the tractor recently he had to stay behind.

But I can't just drive off and leave him; I have to shout at him to 'go and lie down' and he slinks off, looking over his shoulder at me with a look that says 'bastard'.

So I went off without him for the day and when I was returning home several hours later, in a gateway about 100 yards from our farm lane, I could see a little black head looking down the road towards me.

I was still a fair distance away but Mert recognised the tractor and was off towards home down the middle of the road, tail wagging and as pleased as could be to see me.

What could I say? How long had he been there? Doesn't he realise that most of the traffic is doing more than 60? Has he had a copy of *Greyfriar's Bobby* from the library and got the idea of a vigil from that?

I just had to pat him on the head when I got off the tractor and be a bit proud of him.

But the next day I was off to top a field of docks. It's the second crop of docks on that field and I wasn't taking any chances. I put him in his shed, gave him some food and made a fuss of him.

When I finished topping the docks, the cattle in the field followed me to the gate. Despite my best efforts, one of them popped out on to the road as I took the tractor out of the field.

Dilemma! One on the road and 37 in the field trying to join it! Then I could have done with a dog! I stood in the gateway to stop the 37 and waited for help.

After five minutes it arrived in the form of a very attractive lady in an Audi convertible. She wound down her window and asked if I was in trouble. I explained the situation to her and suggested that she get out of her car and run up the road to fetch the heifer back while I stopped the others coming out on to the road.

Fair play, that's what she did, and very fleet of foot she turned out to be, with a smile to go with it.

If the dog and I are a strong couple, the threesome (if you pardon the expression) are the dog and me and the Discovery. It's how we travel about, it's how we go on adventures together, it's how Mert is able to put his head through the window and scare the living daylights out of joggers and cyclists.

The Discovery out on the yard cost me £1,300 three years ago. They've been three hard years and recent events have taken their toll. Most of the windows are now permanently open, which means wet bums for passengers.

The front right wing met a neighbour's pick-up in a lane so the headlight on that side shines about a yard in front of you.

Worse than all that, we are milking our cows three times a day now and the evening milkers have taken to using the Discovery to fetch the cows in.

I don't mind that so much but they leave it parked overnight in a gateway where all the cows travel. Cows like a good rub and a scratch. Half-a-ton of cow having a bit of a rub on a wing or door soon puts a few dents into a panel. If you are a cow and want to have a good scratch, what better than a wing mirror?

Appearance is important for MOT purposes, however. We once had a farm van that failed its MOT because it was mouldy.

The MOT is due at the end of this month. Last year I took it and was told the body underneath needed £700 of welding, besides anything else that needed doing. I took it home to think about it; you have to think about it if that's all it's worth.

I told a friend of mine in the car trade about the dilemma. Lest you should think having a friend in the car trade sounds pretentious, he's a sort of Arthur Daley-type who lives in the countryside – an Arthur Daley with nettles.

He said he would take it and have a look at it. Half a day later it was back, all MOT'd, with just the fee to pay. Obviously he'd got a tame MOT man somewhere, which is alright, but then, of course, it isn't, is it?

So I'm not going to waste time this year. This Discovery will join its predecessor in our nettle patch and out on the yard is yet another replacement – £1,700 this time, but only 10 years old.

It's pristine, with air conditioning and leather upholstery – almost too good to be true!

We've not used it yet (I will tax it at the start of the month), but the dog has already pee'd on all the wheels and we, the dog and I, can't wait to start another round of adventures.

THERE is a man of my acquaintance, for whom I have great regard, who is much given to singing on licensed premises. He has a fine voice, although his repertoire of songs is quite small.

He's a good man to have at a funeral. By and large, the singing at funerals around here is very poor. Move just 10 miles west and the difference is quite remarkable. Around here they don't start standing up until the first word of the first hymn, so most of the first line is lost in the general melee of standing up, clearing the throat and uncertain singing.

I have already determined, should I have the opportunity to make such plans, that at my own funeral the vicar is to announce at the very start that if they, the congregation don't sing the first verse tidily, then we move straight to the interment. I also want to be buried in the garden under a cedar tree, so that my gravestone will be a confounded nuisance to countless future generations of strimmers.

But I return to my friend the singer. He is fairly predictable in his sequence of songs and when we have had two renderings of *Home on the Range* in quick succession, we know he is winding down.

Singing exhausted for the moment, he will try to start a discussion about rats. 'Do you know of any use for a rat?' People usually start to drift away at this juncture because they've heard it all before. It's usually me that stops to listen because I know that with a couple more pints inside him he will get his second wind and we will start off again with *When the Coal comes from the Rhondda*, which is a particular favourite of mine.

As far as I know, no-one has ever answered his question about rats. I've discussed most of the species of wildlife that live around here within these pages, but it is the rat we turn our attention to today. You will have realised by now that we farm where we live and we also have a farmyard a mile or so away that we rent. We mostly keep on top of the rats here at home, partly because my son has bait points all around our poultry unit that he keeps primed, and because the rest of our buildings are over-run with cats.

I sometimes think the cats are more trouble than a population of rats would be but they are more socially acceptable even if they cost me a fortune to feed. On the other hand, the rats at our other farm have been gaining the upper hand.

Rats promote different reactions in different people. If I see one, I'll look for a stick to chase it. My son, who is a strapping lad and well able to look after himself in most situations, is petrified of them. We have our dry cows shut in buildings at the other farm in the winter and his nightly bedtime job is to get into his truck and go to see if the chickens are all right and then drive up to see if there is a cow calving.

He tells me that when he goes to see the cows, there are so many rats about he has to sit in his truck with the engine running until the rats disappear and it's safe to get out.

We have started keeping a four-wheel drive loader up there because we cart quite a lot of silage home from there and if the loader is already there, one person can go and get a load of silage on his own.

Then I had a report that a young driver jumped into the loader one morning and there were four rats under the seat. The mental picture of four rats being disturbed from their slumber, getting up, yawning and stretching before tumbling out of the cab door is one I cherish.

After that, there was a stick left by the loader and various drivers would beat the cab door with a stick before they would get in. I thought it was all very amusing until the rats started eating the wiring while they were in there. It wasn't so funny when I couldn't start the machine.

Time for action, time for rat poison. I put a lot of bait out over four days and it was all eaten. None's gone for two days now, so I suspect it has done its job.

I bought a de luxe turbo sort of bait. 'Kill a dog if it eats some,' said the man behind the counter. There'd be a row if it did.

★ ★ ★

IT'S A QUARTER to four on Sunday morning. We always start just a bit earlier at weekends so we can get the work finished up. I don't want to be working all day at weekends.

The weather forecaster predicted minus five this morning, 'could be colder out in the countryside', which I think is us, and I agree, it *is* colder.

This is the sort of weather my mother warned me about when she tried to persuade me not to be a farmer. 'You get a job in a bank and you'll have a comfortable job for life.' And 'On a farm you'll be out in all weathers, by the time you're getting old, all your joints will be suffering'. And then, as if she knew she was wasting her time, 'You mind you take one of those cod liver oil capsules every day – that'll help'.

Like most mothers, she was right. I am out in all weathers and, yes, my joints are creaking a bit, and, yes, I do take a cod liver oil capsule every day – in a way, it's my way of remembering her and doing what she tells me. I still miss her.

There are two of us on duty this morning, one to milk and me to clean up what has fallen on the floor during the night, what we call slurry, and to do some feeding.

We push the cows into the yard next to the parlour and you can see the breath coming out of all of us. I go to start the small and old tractor we use for this job and it bursts into life instantly. It's 35 years old but we park it in the feed passageway at night and the warmth of the cows keeps the worst excesses of the frost away.

It's not all negatives this morning though, because it is so cold the slurry has the consistency of thick porridge and is much easier to control. I can push it and pull it where I will and it stays nicely together. On wet days it has a mind of its own and will run anywhere – often the little tractor and I have to chase it.

A rat comes by and we chase that instead. I've never run one over but you have to try. I have often managed to cover them with a wave of slurry, which I am sure makes them very popular when they get back down their hole.

That's all I can do for now until the last of the cows have gone into the parlour and I get the loader tractor going, which is also parked in the warm feeding passage, and spend 10 minutes pushing silage back towards cows that have spent most of the night nosing about looking for the best bits so that it has ended up out of reach.

I decide to walk across to the chicken sheds to see if they are OK; a sort of fog hangs over them in what light there is, as the fans pump warm air out in to the cold. The computer in the chicken sheds tells me its 25°C in there but outside it is minus eight. Minus eight! Even in my mother's worst-case scenario she didn't mention minus eight.

I ask the chickens if they'd like to be free-range today. They don't bother to answer but I know how many would come outside if I opened up the door.

This is one of the flaws in the concept of 'free-range is best' because it certainly wouldn't work well in the winter months. The birds would rather stay in the shed all day and still be overcrowded. If I were to give my birds a better life, and I'd like to, I would reduce the numbers in the shed by about a third and give them longer to grow.

Most chicken growers would agree but unless the financial returns from this reduced output were the same as with the intensive regime we have now, it quite simply will not happen. The margins we work on are so minimal that people cannot believe it. If we made 10p a bird it would seem like a fortune and it is frequently less than half that sum. But back on my little tractor, the cold is beginning to get to me. The tractor is now white all over, inside and out, as its got a few windows missing.

When I get into the seat I get a frosty bum.

The parlour is being washed out now and clouds of steam rise off the yard. We use tap water to cool the first few degrees out of the milk and retain that water to wash out, so we are in effect washing out with warm water.

The steam makes it look a bit warmer but it isn't really. Water is cheaper than electricity to start the cooling process, but only just.

I'm not sorry when it's time to start breakfast – there's nothing like beans on toast on a cold morning.

I make myself a cup of tea, open the Rayburn, back up to it slowly and the warmth starts to drive out the cold. It's still not 6.30am, but it's time for my cod liver oil capsule.

My mother was right in her prophecies about the life I would lead as a farmer, but I wouldn't have it another way.

And Miles to Go Before I Sleep
A British Vet in Africa
Hugh Cran £8.99

Innocent Victims
Rescuing the Stranded Animals of Zimbabwe's Farm Invasions
Meryl Harrison £16.99

The Countryman's Bedside Book
by BB / Denys Watkins-Pitchford £18.95

My Animals and Other Family
Phyllida Barstow £16.99

The Byerley Turk
The True story of the First Thoroughbred
Jeremy James £7.99

Manual of a Traditional Bacon Curer
Maynard Davies £25

Maynard: The Adventures of a Bacon Curer
Maynard Davies £9.99

Maynard: The Secrets of a Bacon Curer
Maynard Davies £9.99

Advice from a Gamekeeper
John Cowan £20

That Strange Alchemy
Pheasants, Trout and a Middle-Aged Man
Lawrence Catlow £17.99